Five Cries of

Help for Families on Troublesome Issues

*Merton P. Strommen
and A. Irene Strommen*

HarperSanFrancisco
A Division of HarperCollinsPublishers

FIVE CRIES OF PARENTS. Copyright © 1985, 1993, by Merton P. Strommen and A. Irene Strommen. All rights reserved. Printed in the United States of America. No part of this book may be used or reproduced in any manner whatsoever without written permission except in the case of brief quotations embodied in critical articles and reviews. For information address Harper-Collins Publishers, 10 East 53rd Street, New York, NY 10022.

FIRST HARPERCOLLINS PAPERBACK EDITION PUBLISHED IN 1993

Library of Congress Cataloging-in-Publication Data

Strommen, Merton P.
    Five cries of parents : help for families on troublesome issues /
Merton P. Strommen and A. Irene Strommen.
    p.   cm.
    Includes bibliographical references and index.
    1. Parenting. 2. Parent and Child. 3. Family—Religious life.
4. Youth—Conduct of life. 5. Youth—Religious life. I. Strommen,
A. Irene. II. Title.
HQ755.8.S77 1993
649'.1–dc20   91–59023
                                                                       CIP

93 94 95 96 97 RRD(H) 10 9 8 7 6 5 4 3 2 1

This edition is printed on acid-free paper that meets the American National Standards Institute Z39.48 Standard.

To Kathleen and Gilbert Wrenn
who have been loving surrogate parents
to hundreds of graduate students and their spouses

Contents

List of Figures and Tables

FIGURES

TABLES

Preface

We would like to tell you about ourselves and our family. It may help your understanding of *Five Cries of Parents*.

We are the parents of five sons—Peter, Timothy, James, John and David. Our two eldest sons were adolescents when the last two boys were born. Because of the family age span, we have had adolescents in our home for twenty-two consecutive years. And this means that for twenty-two years we continually had five different stages of development around us.

We know firsthand about the power of peer pressure; the embarrassment of being fifteen and not wanting to be seen in the local ice cream store with your little brother in tow; the feeling of alienation when you get teeth braces the same year you make your debut at the big junior high; the resentment against your parents when you're told you have to say home with the family on Christmas Day instead of spending it at your newest girl friend's house; the desperation you feel when you're thirteen and trying to find your lost dog late at night; the awesomeness of your first brush with death when Grandpa dies; the rage when your brother eavesdrops on the other phone when you're talking to a girl.

We know how parents struggle for the right words when a son bursts with frustration after spending most of the basketball game on the bench; or loses a coveted championship game by a field goal that went over the goal posts after the buzzer sounded; or tears a ligament in his knee and is "out" for the season.

We know the shared sense of joy when a son gets the highest rating in original oratory at the state contest; or gets a lead in the school musical; or is voted Most Valuable Player at the end-of-the-season banquet.

We also know the irritation when brothers quarrel, when the police stop your son for throwing tomatoes at passing cars (from the roof of the church library!); or when a son sits sullenly at family devotions, refusing to participate (the same son, we might add who said not long ago, "Thanks, Mom and Dad, for being so persistent in bringing us the faith"). We know the unease of those first nights that the newly licensed driver drives the family car and parents lie awake waiting for the sound of the garage door closing. We know the exuberation of cramming all seven of us into a station wagon with tent equipment and sleeping bags, bound for vacation in the mountains. We also know about the tired father who wonders how he can make it to the first night's stop without collapsing from fatigue.

And so it follows that the adolescent years in our home have been blessed with the patchwork quilt of much discussion, laughter, competition, celebration, reflection, tenderness. It is because of our "boys" that we dare to write this book. And we thank them publicly here for sharing positive and negative observations about our family life, even giving permission at times to be quoted. Peter, Jim, John, and Dave did a preliminary reading of the manuscript for us. We also thank our three daughters-in-law—Norma Jean, Dawn, and Judy—for their openness and willingness to contribute their insights.

For over twenty years Irene's work world was the high school classroom. During Merton's professional career, he has taught, counseled, and researched adolescents. Our work settings have varied from rural and small-town communities to the urban and suburban areas of our country.

Over a span of twenty-five years we have had the privilege of being leaders of small groups of adolescents. Many of these groups met once a week in the form of a Bible study-discussion in the informal setting of our family room.

The chapters of this book represent the keystones of our personal philosophy of parenting. The promises of God in both the Old and New Testaments, our faith in Christ, and the presence of God's Spirit are a heritage we ourselves have been given and have tried to pass on to our sons.

Though we have worked together on writing assignments for many years, we have never before been co-authors. Naturally, some questions arose: "Will our writing styles mesh?" "Can we write at home where the dining room table is the desk?" "Where can we keep the hundreds of references and thousands of questionnaires?" Although we rented a room in a nearby school for a short time, the bulk of the work has been done in our home. It has indeed been easy to misplace data. In fact, one important file folder of references was found in the garage, slated for the garbage can! There were seemingly endless revisions—to the point where we said to each other, "Will we ever finish?" But now we can truthfully say it has been a rich experience to crystallize into words the thoughts on parenting that have accumulated in our hearts and minds for thirty-seven years.

We thank our extended family, which has always been a positive support to us in our life as parents.

We thank the 8,156 young adolescents and the 10,467 parents who gave the unprecedented information being shared in this book. We thank the thousands who allowed us to interview them through handwritten response or verbal sharing.

We thank the talented and hardworking team at Search Institute that carried out the Adolescent-Parent study, which forms a basic reference throughout the book. The people responsible for this study are: Peter L. Benson, Arthur L. Johnson, Phillip K. Wood, Dorothy L. Williams, and Janice E. Mills.

We thank Lutheran Brotherhood for the use of their computers in carrying out the complex analyses of data supplied by the young adolescents and their parents. We have been the recipient of this generous service over a period of 26 years.

We thank Elizabeth Kurak and Jean Wachs for their typing skills on the word processor.

We thank Andy Horne, and Shelby and Jim Andress for

/   FIVE CRIES OF PARENTS

reviewing preliminary copy and helping us set directions for our revisions.

It is with a special sense of gratitude that we acknowledge the hours spent by C. Gilbert Wrenn in perusing the manuscript carefully several times. His work as consulting editor for this book represents only one of many ways in which he has expressed genuine interest and affection for his former advisee, Merton, and the research he has carried out. Gilbert Wrenn has been a friend, mentor, and father.

A special thanks to Lilly Endowment, Inc. for their generous grant and the thirteen youth-serving national organizations for dedicated involvement in the Adolescent-Parent Survey. Their participation made possible the rich treasury of data that form the foundation of this book.

•

A year after this book was published, we lost Dave, our fifth son, at age 25. Our grief journey is described in the book *Five Cries of Grief*, published in 1993. It shows how powerfully, and at times differently, such an experience impacts the life of each parent and members of the entire family.

1. A Time of Danger and Opportunity

危 = Danger

機 = Opportunity

危 機 = Crisis

We have been parents for almost four decades now. Throughout those years we have uttered each of the five cries discussed in this book.

Because Merton is a research psychologist at Search Institute[1] in Minneapolis, Minnesota, we have had privileged access to a large amount of unique research data, accumulated over twenty-five years. Of special import are the findings of the massive study of Young Adolescents and their Parents, also called the Adolescent-Parent study, which was carried out by Peter L. Benson and the research team of Search Institute in 1983. Supplementing this research are data from a host of other studies, and insights garnered from scores of books and articles on parenting.

This introductory chapter deals with the following topics:

- The five cries
- Danger and opportunity
- Purpose of this book
- Our data base
- Our interpretive stance

The Five Cries of Parents

Parents of adolescent children often have searching and sometimes urgent questions. They want answers that will provide them with insight, guidance, and support. We call these searching questions "cries" because they represent the strong desire of parents for:

- Understanding
- Close family
- Moral behavior
- Shared faith
- Outside help

We also use the concept of cries to underscore just how stressful parenting adolescent children can be. A parent's need for answers during this period is perhaps more urgent than at any other stage in the family life cycle.

In 1983 a comprehensive sociological study of more than one thousand families[2] confirmed something that had been observed in other, smaller, studies: instead of improving over the years as parents gain in experience, there is actually a steady decline in most measures of family achievement from the childless stage to the adolescent-raising stage of the family life cycle. During these years, closeness and adaptability reach a low point, and communication between parents and adolescents is poorest. Where that occurs, one can expect to find a highly stressed family.

In 1984 a smaller study of 208 families[3] came up with similar findings. Virtually all parents view the adolescent stage in family life as the most difficult. Why? One reason is parental annoyance over issues of independence and control. A second reason is parental fears over the potentially undesirable consequences of their child's new-found independence. These fears may relate to drugs, reckless driving, or delinquent behavior. Though parents know they are supposed to encourage and facilitate independence, they find this responsibility difficult to carry out.

Added to the difficulty of managing teenage children is the difficulty of financial support. Today's parents are under increased strain to provide money needed to support and educate their growing children, whose needs grow right along with them. Thus financial and business strains are especially intense during this stage of family life.

Both parent and adolescent are simultaneously in unique cycles of growth and change—children in adolescence, and the parents in what some psychologists call "middlescence," the years between thirty-five and fifty. Gail Sheehy writes that wives past the age of thirty-five often experience a movement toward more independence.[4] During these same years, according to Eda LeShan,[5] the husband may become more aware of unfulfilled aspirations, mistaken decisions and choices, things left undone. He may realize that there will be no "big time" in his career. Hence this period of married life is ripe for anxiety, impatience, and misunderstanding.

Danger and Opportunity

Initially, we considered making "fear" one of the five cries of parents. On closer examination, however, we came to see that fear is not a separate cry, but rather a quality that gives urgency to the others. Parents have many fears because they know how susceptible children and young adolescents are to the social infections of our culture. This fear has been intensified by the many tragic accounts reported daily in the news media.

Another fear is generated by the word "epidemic," a term used increasingly in scholarly journals and popular press. The term refers not to diseases such as smallpox, cholera, yellow fever, or malaria, but to behaviors that are equally devastating to the lives of youth and adults. Almost half of all patients hospitalized today are there not because of a disease, but because of practices that are symptoms of an illness such as drug use, alcoholism, or child abuse. These social ills, all of which have appeared on the horizon as aggravated social problems, are like contagious diseases. They are passed on through peer pressure and through the mass media.

But a time of crisis, with its obvious dangers, can also be a time of opportunity. This awareness is incorporated into the two-part Chinese character for the word "crisis": one part means danger, and the other opportunity.

The response to an epidemic situation can involve three different actions: trying to eliminate the infectious disease, cutting off the ways by which the disease is communicated, and increasing the immunity or health of people through vaccines or improved nutrition. This book stresses the third strategy. There is much that parents can do to counter social infection by increasing the inner strength and immunity of their children.

Our studies have shown that adolescents are vastly helped if they can draw on five great sources of strength:

- Understanding, affirming parents
- Close, caring families
- Moral, service-oriented beliefs
- A personal, liberating faith
- An accepting attitude towards receiving help

Used correctly, they can at least partially deter negative behaviors and encourage a life of service and responsible action. These five sources of strength will be described in later chapters.

This hopeful stance is in tune with the feelings of parents in the Adolescent-Parent study. Though four out of ten parents admit they worry "very much" about their child's future, and an additional three in ten worry "quite a bit," they are still hopeful. When asked to describe their own child, they tended to reflect a positive attitude by a use of words such as "caring," "feeling for others," "happy," "respectful for authority," and "trouble-free." Though some parents described their child as hard to live with or rebellious, such parents are in the minority. Most of the parents in the Adolescent-Parent study enjoy their children and find considerable satisfaction in parenting.[6] This is seen in the responses fathers and mothers gave to the statement "I get a lot of satisfaction out of being a parent."

	Mother	Father
Almost always true	60%	53%
Often true	28%	33%
Combined Answers	88%	86%

These results are noteworthy because family satisfaction strongly indicates a family that is resilient, able to face hardships, and endure stress. A 1986 study of 1,000 families identifies this characteristic with regenerative families—ones that cultivate trust, respect, and maintenance of stability.[7]

In spite of the fear of the future that seems to dominate the media, fewer than one in five parents in the Adolescent-Parent study agrees with the statement "I sometimes wish I did not have children." Though aware of the dangers facing adolescents, parents in the study seem strongly attuned to the opportunities and possibilities of parenting. Whether you think them misguided or not, the fact remains that 85 percent of these parents agree with the statement "I think I'm doing a pretty good job as a parent." This positive attitude can only help them be good parents, able to turn potentially dangerous situations into opportunities for significant growth.

Purpose of This Book

This book is addressed to parents and other adults who are in a parenting role with children and adolescents. Its purpose is to provide a rationale for parenting, to encourage reflection, and to supply clear directions regarding the help parents may need.

We have tried to organize commonly held ideas about parenting into an easily remembered conceptual framework, supplied by the five cries and the essentials of parenting to which they point: understanding, close family, moral purpose, shared faith, and outside help.

We encourage you to reflect on parenting. Poor parenting can result from a parent's unresolved personal problems. There are brilliant psychiatrists and psychologists who know a great deal about the human personality, but are inept as parents. Their insecurities and needs, obvious to others but not to themselves, profoundly influence their actions. Though insightful and effective when helping others, they lose their effectiveness when dealing with issues that touch their own lives. Unresolved dynamics can cause them—as well as anyone—to act contrary to their better knowledge. Having observed this phenomenon again and again, we find it crucial to encourage all parents to reflect on themselves as people and mates, as well as parents. We believe every parent needs to work at examining and understanding his or her hidden feelings. For parents of adolescent children, in a time of stress and change, this is doubly important.

Although this is not a "how-to" book, we hope it will help parents change. Thus each chapter includes practical suggestions culled from interviews, scores of excellent books on parenting, and our own experiences as parents. Use these suggestions as presented, or allow them to help your imagination envision new ways to solve problems.

Our Database

To address the five cries and provide answers not previously available, we have used factual data from a number of studies involving parents. A principal source of information is the aforementioned Adolescent-Parent study, which involved 8,165 young adolescents and their 10,467 parents. This study, funded by Lilly Endowment, was based on thirteen national samples of young adolescents (grades 5 through 9), randomly selected from the membership rosters of thirteen national youth-service organizations (see Table 1 for more information on the sample). All groups used the same questionnaire of 319 items and the same procedures in collecting data. A separate but parallel questionnaire of 328 items was used to query the parents of these adolescents.

Table 1. Sample Sizes and Origins*

	Sample Sizes					
Grade in school	Young Adolescents			Parents		
	Boys	Girls	Total	Mothers	Fathers	Total
5	660	720	1,380			
6	807	852	1,659			
7	866	978	1,844			
8	888	1,010	1,898			
9	586	677	1,263			
Total	3,807	4,237	8,165**	6,076	4,391	10,467

	Sample Origins		
Sponsoring Agency	Percent of Young Adolescent Sample	Percent of Mother Sample	Percent of Father Sample
African Methodist Episcopal Church	3%	1%	2%
American Lutheran Church	10	14	13
Baptist General Conference	7	10	8
Churches of God, General Conference	4	5	5
Evangelical Covenant Church	6	8	7
4-H Extension	14	12	14
Lutheran Church—Missouri Synod	7	9	8
National Association of Homes for Children	7	0	0
National Catholic Educational Association	14	8	10
Presbyterian Church/U.S.	5	7	6
Southern Baptist Convention	8	8	9
United Church of Christ	8	9	9
United Methodist Church	8	10	9

*This table identifies sample sizes and their origins as well as the percentage each contributes to the composite sample. No reference is made in this book to information from any of the individual samples, only the total samples of 8,165 adolescents and 10,467 parents.
**Includes 121 young adolescents, grade or sex unknown.

The study is unprecedented in size of sample, scope of questioning, and specificity of information. Though the results of the composite sample based on these national groups can be applied only to the populations they represent (about 60 percent of the national population), the conclusions shared here have wide application. Care has been taken to find corroborative data (based on samples of the general public) to justify the making of generalizations that will apply to parents generally.

As a preliminary to the Adolescent-Parent study, we asked approximately two thousand parents to respond to a questionnaire consisting of thirty item stems, such as the following:

The worst thing about my family is _____ .
When my child does something wrong, I _____ .
I would be a better parent if _____ .
The best thing about our family is _____ .

Many parents wrote freely, describing their hopes, dreams, and difficulties. From these brief essays we extracted quotes to illustrate the thoughts and feelings that underlie the statistics used in this book.

In addition to reading the questionnaire results, we interviewed approximately two hundred young and older adults, as well as some high school youth. We asked them such questions as:

Describe the most important qualities in the parent you yourself want to be.

Describe your most positive experience as an adolescent in your home.

If you could change one quality of your home life as an adolescent, what would it be?

We were impressed by the comments of the people we interviewed, for they included many insights similar to those found in books written for parents. While they often acknowledged mistakes and failures, the interviewees seemed to know what constitutes good parenting.

Though this book is truly data based, it is not a research report. Rather, it represents our interpretation of the meaning inherent in a mosaic of research findings. We have used the data to broaden our understanding and increase our ability to see with clarity the significance of what parents and adolescents report about their families.

It should be noted that we have added findings drawn from two major studies conducted in 1990. The first is a national study of youth and adults in 561 randomly selected congregations of six Protestant denominations (United Methodist, Presbyterian USA, Evangelical Lutheran, Church in America, Christian Church, Southern Baptist, and United Church of Christ). The study, *Effective Christian Education: A National Study of Protestant Congregations*, yields new information on what it is that encourages faith and loyalty in youth and adults.[8]

The second study is a survey of 47,000 students (grades 6–12) found in 111 communities in 25 states. Entitled *The Troubled Journey: A Profile of American Youth*, this study presents new information on factors that deter youth from involvement in at-risk behaviors.[9]

These studies add to this book by both confirming and giving greater currency to the Adolescent-Parent study.

Our Interpretative Stance

Admittedly, our interpretations are biased by our values, beliefs, and personal experiences. As Christians, we reflect a distinct value orientation and world view. But the research findings on which our conclusions are based provide a measure of objectivity. They help to establish our basic points as something more than personal opinion.

As authors, we believe that each source of strength within the family contributes to the growth and development of an adolescent. We also believe that a liberating religious faith enhances each characteristic. We use the word "liberating" faith because our studies evidence two types: a forgiveness-oriented faith and a guilt-oriented faith. One is freeing and the other enslaving.

A liberating Christian faith fosters love and trust within a family; it encourages an open, understanding, affirming stance toward oneself and others. This openness makes it easier to accept help, acknowledging that supportive people, trained counselors, and studies on "parenting the adolescent" are all gifts of God.

In conclusion, we feel it is essential to emphasize that parenting is an ongoing process that begins at a child's birth. Each source of strength mentioned here, developed more fully throughout the book, has its roots in the early stages of family life. This means that preparation for the adolescent years begins in childhood. And parenting never ends. Though the role we play will change, as parents we are always parents. The umbilical cord is truly cut only when death separates us from our children.

In Letty Cottin Pogrebin's words, "If the family were a sport, it would be baseball: a long, slow nonviolent game that is never over until the last out."[10]

2. Cry for Understanding Yourself As a Parent

> If you cry out for insight and raise your voice for *understanding*, if you seek it like silver and search for it as for hidden treasure . . . wisdom will come into your heart and *understanding* will guard you.
>
> —PROVERBS 2:3, 10

Parents of two thoughtful children decided to invite a child from another culture and contrasting style of life into the warmth of their family. The eight-year-old Asian girl they adopted had been a procurer for her mother, whose livelihood came from serving as a prostitute for U.S. servicemen.

To understand their adopted daughter better, the parents met with others who had adopted Asian children. They read books and consulted with friends. Soon they observed that two personalities were embattled within the girl—one that responded to the love and caring of her new home and congregation, and one that wanted her former style of life. The latter attraction drew her toward people who were glad to exploit her. By the time she was in junior high, she was using drugs and sexually active.

"How can we help her to break with friends and practices that are destroying her future?" cried this girl's new parents. They visited school counselors and pastoral counselors, they read books—all in their search for insight and understanding. Over time, their persistent cry became, "How can we best parent a daughter whose childhood experiences are the determining force in her life?"

In their search for wisdom these parents discovered not only need for a better understanding of their child, but also of themselves as people and of each other as mates. As a result they joined Al-Anon and became a part of a parents' group with its weekly discussions.

This chapter takes a look at the forces and dynamics that influence our perception and response as parents within a family situation. They are the key to understanding adolescent behavior, which is the focus of the next chapter.

This chapter is divided into two sections.

- The emotional forces that move out of our past and into the present: forces from our family of origin; wounded memories; unmet personal needs; feelings of failure; and reactions of anger.
- The emotional forces that are intensified by stressful circumstances in a marriage situation: external trauma, such as death in the family; divorce and separation; single parenting; and establishing a step-family.

The Need for Understanding Hidden Emotional Dynamics

When the 10,467 parents in the Adolescent-Parent study were asked to rank the importance of sixteen values, two that received top billing were "to be a good parent" and "to have wisdom (mature understanding, insight)." The high ranking of wisdom and understanding does not seem to be an idle desire, but one that is matched by an awareness of its challenge. Four out of five parents agreed that "to be a good parent is one of the hardest things in life I do."

In other words, parents in the study do want to receive insight into the character and subtleties of their adolescent sons and daughters. They do want to grasp the meaning of their children's often cutting remarks and puzzling reactions. They do want to know when discipline is too severe or too lenient. They do want to be able to communicate better with their adolescent children.

Interestingly, however, the parents in the Adolescent-Parent study tend to minimize their own personal difficulties. True, some do admit they have problems in relating to others. Some do characterize themselves as very emotional, not able to devote themselves completely to others, very competitive, not at all kind, insensitive to the feelings of others, troubled with feelings of inferiority, or likely to go to pieces under pressure. But the number who thus describe themselves is few indeed.

The majority of parents characterize themselves as active, gentle, kind, confident, and warm in their relations with others. Fathers especially tend to see themselves as independent, able decision makers who stand up well under pressure. While they feel that they are less able than mothers to devote themselves completely to other people, they still see themselves as strongly helpful and "somewhat" aware of the feelings of others.

Mothers characterize themselves as quite emotional and at times prone to go to pieces under pressure. But they also stress that they are able to devote themselves "completely" to others, are highly aware of people's feelings, and are very warm in their interpersonal relationships.

One might conclude that the chief need for parents is to gain a better understanding of their children. This is important, but as parents we also need to get in better touch with our own feelings and those of our mate. There is an interrelationship between such disturbing questions as, "Why the antagonism between my son and me?" and the question, "Why does my mate overreact during a family crisis?"

Though parents may sense it, they seldom verbalize the truth that hidden dynamics do affect their behavior. One reason is that we can never be fully in touch with our feelings, drives, or motivations. Even parents trained in the area of human relations are not always aware of the emotional forces that cause them to treat their children insensitively. An emotional dynamic can subtly cloud the understanding of the most loving and insightful parent. The result is an inability to see that certain actions are inappropriate and even at times hurtful.

Family of Origin

Our family of origin determines much of what we do as parents. Recall, for instance, times when you have stopped in your tracks and realized you were reacting just as your own mother or father used to do when you were a child.

A friend says, "Whenever I get hurt and angry and I sense myself withdrawing in silence to lick my wounds, I say to myself, 'Don't do it. Remember how you hated when Mother did that.'" Another says thoughtfully, "What can I do about this habit of yelling at my kids? I don't really believe that's the way to handle a situation, but it was the way Mom did it at home. It frightens me a little when I think my children will do the same unless I change."

A 1983 *Time* magazine article on violence in the home spoke of the powerful dynamics that are established by abusive parents.[1] "Like a poisonous plant sending out spores," family violence tends to reproduce itself. Battered children grow up disposed to batter their own offspring. (See Chapter 7 for a fuller discussion on this subject.) As parents, we need to recognize the power of our family of origin—to be aware of its negative and positive patterns of behavior and their potential for continuing to shape our behavior. We may need consciously to break certain negative patterns and discipline ourselves to act otherwise. Of course, we may also try consciously to emulate some of the positive behaviors and attitudes our parents modeled so beautifully.

Wounded Memories

These memories are the hurtful remembrances of our past that still influence us today. Sigmund Freud dramatized the enduring power of early experience by showing how the effect of traumatic childhood experiences lingers on into adulthood. Our past experiences and decisions profoundly affect our present perceptions as parents and mates. For this reason, in a marriage relationship, mothers and fathers need to take time to recall and share experiences of their own youth with each other. Sometimes the memory of an experience helps us understand more clearly our present concerns, as was the case of the counselor in the following illustration.

Tom, a middle-aged man active in the ministry of counseling delinquent boys in a large private school, was in one of our study groups in which members were asked to reminisce about life in their parental home. "Think back on what life was like at dinner time when you were fifteen," they were asked. Tom was initially skeptical of the exercise; but as others contributed to the discussion, he became increasingly pensive. When his turn came to share, he spoke with a touch of sadness. "I had forgotten how much trouble I caused my parents when I was fifteen. It was a bad year."

Sometimes a painful memory of the past helps us respond sensibly in the present.

A soft-spoken elderly woman in our study group cringed when she remembered herself as a girl of fourteen, shouting angrily at her parents, "I'd like to kill you!" But because she remembered, she could understand when similar words came from her grandchild.

However, emotional reactions from the past are not always positive. Sometimes these wounded memories remain within us as negative forces, to cloud our perceptions. Knowing this, a parent who has unhappy memories would do well to discuss them with a professional counselor. Such a step becomes especially important if the experiences have included sexual abuse, or ill treatment by an alcoholic parent. The tragedy of these experiences is their tendency to be lived out again in the life of the child-turned-parent.

Unmet Personal Needs

Related to the dynamic of wounded memories is the emotional force generated by certain unmet personal needs or unfulfilled ambitions. In more than a biological way, children are extensions of their parents. When we as parents begin to live out our ambitions or unfulfilled dreams through them, we can become prey to emotional upheaval for each mistake or inadequacy of our child. Unless the dynamic of our own unmet need is understood, the force brought into play can cause a cleavage between us and our adolescent. Let's look at some illustrations.

Most of us are familiar with the "Babe Ruth" father, who continually shouts his instructions and reprimands to a son at second base. Those sitting beside the father on the bleachers cringe for the boy, to say nothing of his embarrassed mother. This father feels that *he* is out on the field making the mistakes that caused *him* to be cut from the team when *he* was a ninth grader.

Then there is the mother who wanted to excel scholastically in her adolescent years, and often felt inferior because she did not do as well as a brother and sister. Now she pushes her teenage daughter to get As in school. Reprimanded for not having As on her report card, the girl—who actually is an earnest student, though not able to come up to the parents' standards—says, with considerable insight, "I can't understand why you expect *me* to get such good grades. *You* didn't."

What about the father who rebelled against his parents in his youth? As an adult, he regrets this and realizes how much his attitude during his teen years is now tied to many unfulfilled dreams and aspirations. Now he desperately tries to keep his son from taking the same path. But the tactics he uses are heavy-handed, and, as a result, the element of trust is rapidly eroding between father and son.

Feelings of Failure

Though the feeling of having failed as a parent is at some time present within every father and mother, for many parents it is a persistent thought. For about half of the 10,467 parents in the Adolescent-Parent study, "I am not as good a parent as I should be" is a nagging thought. The greatest concern of most parents is that they will fail as parents. Of the fourteen worries listed in the survey, none draws as high a rating as the worry over "the job I am doing in raising this child."

Much of our self-esteem as parents is linked to the behavior of our children. We tend to interpret their failures as our failures. This dynamic, with its accompanying sense of guilt and self-blame, surfaced as a prominent element in the cluster of family concerns among American Lutheran Church women in a 1981 study.[2] It is sufficiently strong and widely enough felt to have caused the following items to cluster together:

1. I am sometimes too harsh in the discipline of my children.
2. I feel unable to cope with my children.
3. My children are not turning out as well as I had hoped they would.
4. My children aren't learning much in school.
5. My husband is sometimes harsh in his discipline of our children.

The power of this dynamic is shown also in its lingering effects on women years after the children have left home. Women over sixty-five are most plagued with these nagging regrets particularly if they are also widows.

Parents who have always been self-critical and troubled with feelings of low self-esteem are especially susceptible to this dynamic. They continue to be sensitive about their modest achievements and their self-perceived limited importance in the scheme of things. Such parents often will react strongly when their children fail to obey or show them proper respect, because they interpret this as another sign of failure. Such parents then tend to become more controlling and rule-oriented. When they have a flare-up with their adolescent child, these parents do not see that their reaction of wanting to punish might be a way of making up for their own feelings of inferiority. Over-strictness and overprotection are control reactions of parents fearful of failure. For how many parents is this especially real? Among the parents of adolescents in the Adolescent-Parent study, it is real for one in four.

Reactions of Anger

Involved in a parent's sense of guilt and failure is regret over having gotten angry. Half of the parents in the Adolescent-Parent study acknowledge that "once in a while" they punish their child more than he or she deserves. One in three admit to times when "I get so angry I might hurt my child." It should be noted that the parents who admit to these outbursts of anger are primarily church-related, conscientious people who very much want to be good parents. David Mace has some insightful statements that apply to both parents and adolescents in family relationships:

The failure to achieve love and intimacy is almost always due to the inability of the persons to deal creatively with anger. Marriage and family living generates in normal people more anger than they experience in any other social situation in which they habitually find themselves. The overwhelming majority of family members know of only two ways of dealing with anger—to vent it or to suppress it. Both of these methods are destructive.[3]

The first way Mace indicates of handling anger—to vent it—is the experience of the father who writes about an incident concerning his eighth-grade daughter:

The children were arguing back and forth. I said to stop but she wouldn't. I got upset and hit her on the side of her head. I wish I had not done it.

This kind of reaction only produces guilt.

A second way of handling anger is to suppress it. Psychologist Haim Ginott in *Between Parent & Teenager* makes an apt observation on this method.[4] He stresses that parents should not convey hypocrisy by being outwardly "nice" while feeling angry inside. Children are very sensitive to parents' reactions and may often sense anger, even when the parents themselves are not fully aware of it.

Ginott contends that anger "should bring some relief to the parent, some insight to the teenager, and no harmful after-effects to either of them."[5] There might be a harmful after-effect if, for example, children are disciplined in front of their friends. The father of an eighth-grade boy writes of this experience: "When my child does something wrong, I get angry and often embarrass him in front of his friends." Such actions only make the child act up more.

Ginott says that parents may effectively express their feelings of anger to an adolescent if they are able to acknowledge the following truths:[6]

1. We accept the fact that in the natural course of events teenagers will make us uncomfortable, annoyed, irritated, angry, and furious.
2. We are entitled to these feelings without guilt or shame or regret.
3. We are entitled to express these feelings with one limitation: No matter how angry we are, we do not insult teenagers' personality or character.

In a situation that creates anger, the parents should first explain to the adolescent what he or she has done wrong and how it makes the parent feel. The parent then needs to tell the teenager what has to be done to correct the situation.

If these steps are followed, the storm clouds evaporate much more easily. A parent does not want to perpetuate waves of anger, defiance, retaliation, and revenge. These can lead to some of the most serious problems in parent-adolescent relationships.

We have seen some of the hidden dynamics that can cause a parent to overreact in a way that surprises both the parent and child. The reaction may be out of proportion to the significance of the incident. A parent may get very angry, or very depressed—withdrawing into a lonely and self-condemning silence that the family senses, but does not understand.

Because these dynamics are usually hidden and not available for personal reflection, a parent needs help to bring these feelings to the surface. There is no substitute for times of conversation and reflection in which husband and wife, parent and pastor, or parent and counselor sit and talk. The amazing phenomenon of unthreatened and reflective conversation is that it provides the setting within which memories of the past can float to the top. These, when explored, may provide insight and release.

Understanding Your Marriage Situation

The dynamics that stem from one's family of origin, from wounded memories, unmet personal needs, feelings of failure, and reactions of anger may be intensified by a stressful marriage situation. Our disappointing personal reactions cannot be fully understood without taking this into consideration.

Stress has the power to worsen relationships between husband and wife or between parent and child. Because certain marriage situations create added stress, consideration will be given here to their possible effects.

Stress-Creating Circumstances

Parents in the Adolescent-Parent study were asked to name the stress-producing situations that have occurred in their family within the life-span of their adolescent son or daughter. They experienced the following stressful situations:

21%	Losing a job
18%	A parent having a serious accident or illness
16%	Severe financial hardship in the family
12%	Parents divorcing
11%	Parents separating
7%	A natural disaster that damaged or destroyed the home, farm, or crops
6%	A parent or child developing a disability or handicap
6%	A family member being arrested
3%	Death of a child

Although only a small percentage (3 percent) of the parents

reported the stress of having lost a son or daughter, we are using the example of a death in the family to show how external pressure may intensify the home situation. The same dynamics are often present in other stressful situations, particularly those in which a child "fails" a parent, as in the case of parents with children who are drug addicts.

Trauma of Death in the Family

In 1976 David M. Kaplan and a research team conducted a study of the impact on 40 families of losing a child to leukemia.[7] They found that within a year after the death, 70 percent of the parents showed evidence of serious marital problems. Forty percent of the families had a parent with a serious drinking problem, and 43 percent of the mothers showed significant difficulty in performing homemaking duties. Obviously, the trauma of the situation had negatively affected the parents. In almost all cases, the study reports that negative effects could have been lessened by better communication between husband and wife, situations where each was allowed into the other's thought life, feelings, and judgments. In this way an environment of safety would have been created, and no one would need to bury an experience for fear it would not be accepted.

Three common factors may hinder communication in this type of situation:

1. The *sense of guilt* parents feel as they endlessly think, "If only I had done this . . . " or "if only I hadn't done that . . . "
2. The *escape into a fantasy world*, imagining that everything is as it used to be.
3. The *use of drugs or alcohol* or both to blank out pain.[8]

The great need is for husband and wife to talk about what has happened and to share each other's pain. It is important that they do this immediately and as an ongoing practice. By talking about loss, the father and mother gain a healthy understanding of how each is bearing the grief. If they do not, two people who have lived together for many years may misunderstand each other's reactions and grow apart.

Because many men in our culture think they are not expected to show emotion (except perhaps anger), it is common for a man in grief to bury it by becoming preoccupied with his work. The wife may think he is uncaring, because he seldom speaks about the child who has died or "failed." On the other hand, the husband may become upset with his wife's reaction of depression, or her constant talking about what has happened.

A helpful structure for promoting communication between spouses after a stressful situation, such as the death of a child, is to set up the following type of family meeting:[9]

1. Let discussion be open-ended, allowing time for "all there is to say."
2. State the intention and willingness to hear the other express feelings.
3. Let one person talk until he or she has said all he or she wants, with no rebuttal.
4. Invite each person to tell what kind of support he or she wants from the other.
5. Make sure there are no interruptions, such as phone or doorbell.

After this period of communication, and a time for husband and wife to spend some time alone together, parents need to give each other space to process and integrate what has happened in their own individual lives during this stress period.

Divorce and Separation

Grief and shock, fear of the future, resentment, self-pity, frustration, and even rage are some of the emotions that cloud the perceptions of divorcing or divorced parents. These emotions place a separated parent under unusual pressures. In a pending marital breakup, parents often fear talking about the situation, so they avoid explaining to their children what is happening. This silence in turn creates fear and guilt feelings in the adolescent. Some parents subject their children to frightening confrontations and displays of verbal abuse, using their children as confidants, spies, and emotional pawns.

Parents can change this situation if they realize that their lack of cooperation is depriving their child of a vital relationship. If they care about the child, separating parents will seek a new framework for dealing with each other as people and a new framework for raising their children. A key element in this working relationship is forgiveness of the former spouse for past unhappiness. With that as the basis, the chances for success are multiplied. Once the trauma of an unhappy marriage is over, divorcing parents may be more free to become good parents. A friend, in reflecting on her divorce, had this to say: "I consider it of prime importance that I do not hate my former husband. If I should hate him, I know my daughters would develop feelings against men and it might affect their future marriages and homes."

As a beginning step, divorcing parents should sit down with their children and explain what is happening and how it will affect each of them. A strong affirmation of parental love is necessary at this time. Parents should not blame each other; and they should stress that the children are not to blame for the divorce, that they are free to love both parents, and that they will not be asked to take sides against either parent. Preteens—nine- to 12-year-olds—are especially vulnerable to being used as an ally by one parent against the other, and may become extremely angry at the parent they feel is to blame. Some children may react physically to this kind of stress, developing stomach aches, headaches, or asthma attacks. Other children may begin to steal or lie. Teenagers often act out anger at their parents by spending more time way from home; some become involved in sexual activity.

Children do not believe in no-fault divorce. They blame one or both parents, or they blame themselves. The need for understanding is great. But with the search for understanding comes the wisdom and insight that has enabled many divorced parents to establish close relationships with their children and enjoy a happy family life.

Single Parents

Because little is known about characteristics that tend to typify single parents, we made a special analysis comparing the responses of 482 single parents to those of parents of intact families (where there has not been separation, divorce, or death).[10] This information may help single parents realize how many of their parenting problems are intensified by their marital situation and not necessarily by poor parenting. It may also help family, friends, and support groups understand what the single parent is having to cope with. Such understanding can lead to supportive action.

Without question, the cry for understanding is strongest from those who valiantly try to be both father and mother. Single parents especially want to know how to communicate better with children, how to instill healthy concepts of what is right and wrong, and how to deal with the practice of drug use. Because their need is so strong, they are more likely than parents of intact families to seek out a specialist for help.

From the standpoint of numbers alone, single parents are a significant group. Approximately half (48 percent) of public school children in the Minneapolis, Minnesota, school system in 1983–84 came from homes with a single parent. A medium-sized city in California reported 63 percent of single-parent homes within the school system. With the divorce rate approaching 50 percent for those now marrying, there should be no decline in the percentage of children who will live, for a time at least, in a single-parent home.

Though every situation is different, certain characteristics do typify single parents. In 90 percent of divorces, children are assigned to the mother's care. For this reason, our findings deal with the mother's situation as single parent. Only one-third of these mothers receive any financial support from the absent mate. As a result, they become involved in downward economic mobility. Some move to more modest housing, often to another community; if they had not done so before, they must now take on full-time jobs. Thus their children suffer multiple losses—loss of father; loss of mother to a heavy work schedule; and often loss of the home, community, and former school friends. Needless to say, the burden such a mother assumes is enormous, not least because of the effect it has on the children.

One single-parent mother, speaking about her eighth-grade daughter's reactions to the divorce, says, "When we moved and changed schools, she went to pieces. All she did was cry and get sick—she missed eighteen days of school in three months. Before, she had perfect attendance. Her inability to adjust upset me. I sought professional counseling. We moved back to our old school district." It is in stressful situations such as these that the cry for understanding becomes a cry of desperation.

When single parents are asked, "How are things going for you and your family these days?" fewer than those of two-parent families in the Adolescent-Parent study are able to answer, "Fairly well" or "Very well." More of them feel their family life is having negative effects on their child, that "members of my family do not get along well with each other." Many more are worried about the job they are doing in raising their child. More single parents rate their child in the direction of being disobedient, rebellious, likely to get into trouble, disrespectful of authority, and not a good student. When trying to imagine what their child worries about, they are more likely (than married mothers) to assume their child has thoughts of suicide and worries about getting beaten up at school or losing a parent through death. Even worse, more think their child is worried about losing parental love, losing the parent to alcoholism, or being physically hurt by the parent.

Some single parents are very conscious of their inability to discipline their children. More often than married mothers, single parents in the Adolescent-Parent study will use extreme measures—either being too lenient when discipline is needed, or reacting in anger by yelling or hitting the child.

Mother-Son Conflict. Understanding and special consideration are needed where there is conflict between mother and son in a single-parent household. A number of studies have found that boys fare worse than girls in a single-parent home, and the negative effects seem to increase with age. This observation was confirmed through a large and comprehensive national study conducted by Guidibaldi in 1983 that compared the children of divorced parents with those in intact families.[11] It documents, for instance, that fifth-grade boys contrast strikingly with fifth-grade girls on a variety of measures. The boys show less peer popularity; greater pessimism; lower scores in reading, math, and classroom conduct; and greater likelihood to repeat a school grade. The contrasts are even more dramatic when boys of divorced parents are compared with girls of divorced parents and with boys of intact families. The consistent finding is that a boy in a single-mother family is more likely to be involved in aggressive acts toward his mother. The findings show that boys typically react with aggression to the stress of divorce, while girls tend to react by being more helpful than before. A single mother, writing about her fifth-grade son, says,

I was divorced when my son was five years old. When he has a problem, he seems to clam up and won't talk. He doesn't listen, and I have to tell him over and over to do something. I wish I knew why he defies me. He has been having a lot of difficulty with schoolwork and getting along with others. He seems to do things deliberately to get punished.

A surrogate father may provide the stabilizing ingredient needed by a fatherless boy. It is impressive to see how the attention and regular contact of a grandfather, uncle, or divorced father can bring about positive changes in an adolescent boy.[12]

Father-Daughter Reaction. It is generally observed that girls do not show the marked negative effects of single parenting found in boys. Nevertheless, the sense of loss is also powerful for girls.

One negative behavior found more often for high school girls living with a single-parent mother is a higher than normal desire for male affection. Such girls are especially vulnerable to the sexual advances of males. With mother gone all day to work, the empty house can become an attractive place for after-school lovemaking. The support of family, friends, congregation, or youth group may form a substitute family that supplies the missing elements of human love and care that adolescents need so desperately when only one parent is in the home.

Loss of Support Systems. A big void in single parenthood is the loss of social support systems. Following divorce, the single mother often significantly decreases her contacts and those of her children with the former husband's relatives. This means breaking relationships with grandparents, aunts, and uncles, who may still care a great deal about the children and mother. There may also be a sharp dropoff in the mother's former friendships, and hence a limited social life.

The 482 single parents who participated in the Adolescent-Parent study showed themselves to be less active in church and less involved in community organizations than intact families. This lack of involvement also holds true for their children. One divorced mother says,

Our family had always been active in church. My husband and I had even been youth leaders for a while. After our divorce, the children (all adolescents) didn't want to participate in church activities anymore. They felt strange and different, as though people no longer liked them and they didn't belong.

The tendency for single parents to withdraw from community institutions is seen in the fact that no more than one out of ten in the Adolescent-Parent study was a single parent (in a day when almost half of public school children are from single-parent homes). This disengagement from congregations, which are potentially important support systems, has been documented elsewhere. Most single parents do not identify with a religious institution.

The lack of adequate support systems places an added burden on the single parent. Perhaps this explains why single mothers are more often drawn to the emotional extremes of slapping, spanking, or yelling at their children. It also may explain why children of single parents find it harder to get along with each other and the parent with whom they live.

From his study, Guidibaldi provides some fascinating data on the importance of support systems.[13] He finds that children of divorced parents fare best in smaller schools—either private or parochial—and ones that use a traditional rather than open classroom structure. Children in these schools demonstrate better classroom adjustment and performance in school environments characterized as "safe, orderly, and predictable." Apparently, such classrooms operate as support systems.

Furthermore, he found that academic performance is significantly higher for children whose grandparents live nearby and are often around to assist with household tasks. The same is true for the children who are in continued contact with the relatives of their custodial parent. Where there is continued contact with relatives and friends among children of divorced parents, one is likely to find more independent learning, less irrelevant talk in the classroom, less withdrawn behavior, less blaming, and less inattention.

It is hard to overstate the benefit to single parents of being surrounded by a group of loving and concerned friends and relatives.

Stepparenting

Far less is known about the pressures common to stepfamilies than to single parents and divorcing parents. However, due to the great increase in divorce and remarriage, stepfamilies represent a growing phenomenon in our country. When single parents marry, each with children from a previous marriage, a new family unit emerges. Puzzling dynamics often operate in the new family situation, ones that make the parents cry out for understanding. As a result, there has been a burgeoning of support and study groups on this area of family life.

What does a father do, for instance, when his stepson views him as an intruder and the person responsible for his parents' break-up? The stepson may be intent on gaining revenge for the hurt he has suffered; he may refuse to go anywhere with his stepfather, or even to carry on a conversation with him. He may react negatively to whatever his stepfather does.

Likewise, it is not rare for a stepparent to have mixed, if not hostile, feelings toward a stepchild, especially if the child exhibits negative characteristics of the divorced mate. A woman referring to her eighth-grade stepdaughter says, "I don't like her. She has the same characteristics of her mother, the ones that caused the divorce in the first place." In the next breath, the same woman speaks of how guilty this attitude makes her feel.

Sometimes a child feels it would be disloyal to like the stepparent. One woman expresses this when she writes of her fifth-grade stepdaughter, "She is torn between me and her real mother."

Equally painful for the stepparent is the situation in which the adolescent feels rejected by the absent parent. "I need help," says one woman, "with a stepson who has been rejected by his father."

A review of current studies led Jolliff to conclude that "though the bonds between stepchildren and stepparents are seldom as strong as those between members of primary families, they can be quite positive and meaningful."[14] He reports that the effect of remarriage is least significant (negatively) for children under the age of eight, somewhat more significant for children between eight and twelve, and the most significant for adolescents.

If the stepparent has a child of his or her own, guilt feelings may arise over loving this child more than the stepchild. It is easy to feel, especially if one has gone through a painful divorce situation, "My poor child has gone through so much trauma. I must do everything I can to make up for it." It is not difficult to see where siding with one's own child in a conflict situation may cause problems with one's mate. This is why the husband-wife relationship is to be treated as primary.

Maturity and leadership are two qualities stepparents need in the "new" family. In trying to understand the stepchild, the new parent needs to recognize that the child probably has feelings of anger toward both stepparent and birth parent, and feelings of guilt over having caused or having failed to stop the divorce. The absent parent tends to be idealized and bad things forgotten. For the child, it is a struggle even to know what name to call the stepparent. But no matter how complex the dynamics, the child still longs to be accepted and to have a happy home, and the stepparent must never forget this.

When children of two families live in the same home, periodically or permanently, it is essential for parents to spend time together—alone. Difficult as this may be with the multiple duties of stepparents, it is of paramount importance. There are unusual stresses on the relationship of husband and wife in remarriage where there is a merging of two families. Therefore, times of sharing problems, learning to know and understand each other, placing priority on the relationship, may mean the difference between a marriage that works out or one that eventually dissolves. (Jolliff stresses, however, that issues of negative behavior are often part of a short-term adjustment, and overconcern can sometimes turn the situation into a long-term adjustment.)

C. Gilbert Wrenn, in *The World of the Contemporary Counselor*, has advice applicable to stepparents. The adolescent, he reminds us, is not a different person because he or she is in a new circumstance. Therefore, he or she should be treated normally, always with a positive emphasis on the future, not on the should-have-beens.[15]

This chapter has addressed the kinds of pressures that affect our ability to be the parent we want to be. In writing this book we have been impressed by how easily most parents can describe the characteristics of good parenting. Yet, the same parents exhibit attitudes and actions that contradict their ideals.

As indicated in the beginning of this chapter, the tendency of parents is not to acknowledge family or personal weaknesses or difficulties. This may be due to an attempt to be a tower of strength for the children, or a hidden desire to appear successful in child rearing. Whatever the reason, parents need to acknowledge that they fight the same battle as their children. They grapple with many of the same issues and want significance and recognition, just as their children do. In coming to understand themselves, they are better able to understand their adolescents. The developmental tasks identified for adolescents in Chapter 3 may be applied equally to parents.

3. Cry for Understanding Your Adolescent

It's hard to rebel when I know you're trying to understand me.

—TEENAGER TO PARENT

A MOTHER'S DIARY

I'm puzzled tonight—and a little bit scared. Up to now—Karen's just going into seventh grade—she's been a delightful girl to have around. She's a fun person and I've always thought she enjoyed being with her Dad and me.

I've tried to tell myself I'm getting too sensitive, but she really hurt me yesterday when she didn't want to go with us to see Grandma. For years we've done this on Sunday afternoons and Karen has loved it. She is her Grandma's pet.

But I distinctly heard her saying to her best friend, Cathy, "You know my mom—she wants me to go along *everywhere* she and Dad go. It's so boring. Sometimes I can hardly *stand* it." (We *don't* go everywhere together—it's only on Sunday afternoons!)

Then she's started wearing her hair like Cathy—long and untidy, and she has such pretty hair when it's neat and combed. But when I said something about it to her the other day, she flared right up at me.

She *knows* how I feel about that loud, awful music she plays when she comes home from school—just when I'm back from work and tired. Sometimes I ask her to *please* turn it down. The last time I did that she snapped back at me in a scornful tone of voice that made me want to cry,

"You're so old-fashioned I can't believe it!"

As parents, we need two pieces of equipment to help us know and understand our adolescents: one, a simple conceptual framework to help us understand the changes typical of this stage of growth; and two, listening skills to help us tune in and discover who our adolescent is and where he or she is in the maturing process.

Framework for Understanding Early Adolescence

A method of organizing our observations will provide a basis for evaluating the significance of what we see and hear as we live with our adolescent children. We need a framework for answering such questions as, "Is this behavior typical of a young adolescent or not?" "What constitutes 'normal, healthy growth'?"

We also need a framework for helping our adolescent answer such questions as, "Who am I?" "How should I understand the puzzling feelings I have?"

These questions relate to the developmental process experienced by every adolescent. Should a young person not progress through the stages of the maturing process, he or she might physically become an adult, but remain a teenager emotionally.

Following are the seven goals an adolescent intuitively seeks to achieve during the teen years.[1]

1. *Achievement.* The satisfaction of arriving at excellence in some area of endeavor.
2. *Friends.* The broadening of one's social base by having learned to make friends and maintain them.
3. *Feelings.* The self-understanding gained through having learned to share one's feelings with another person.
4. *Identity.* The sense of knowing "who I am," of being recognized as a significant person.
5. *Responsibility.* The confidence of knowing "I can stand alone and make responsible decisions."
6. *Maturity.* Transformation from a child into an adult.
7. *Sexuality.* Acceptance of responsibility for one's new role as a sexual being.

The initial letters of each catchword in this list form the acronym "AFFIRMS." Because a conceptual framework may be easily forgotten, using the word "Affirms" as a memory jog can help recall the *seven goals of adolescence*, as follows:

Adolescent Goals

A	Achievement realized
F	Friends gained
F	Feelings understood
I	Identity established
R	Responsibility accepted
M	Maturity gained
S	Sexuality understood

One of these goals is the overall goal of which the other six are parts. The goal of maturity encompasses all the others. We include it as a reminder that our ultimate goal is to see our child become a responsible, caring adult.

We have chosen "Affirms" as a key word because our studies of the helping professions show the concept to be of high importance in working with people. Search Institute carried out a large study for the Association of Theological Schools that involved over 4,000 clergy and lay members randomly selected from 47 denominations. One purpose of the study was to determine the criteria people use when evaluating the effectiveness of pastor, priest, or rabbi.

An open and affirming approach to people ranked highest in importance, irrespective of denomination. This style of relating to people, a pastor's most important quality in ministry, includes the following elements:

1. Remains positive and affirming to people even when handling stressful situations
2. Is willing to acknowledge own limitations and personal mistakes
3. Shows a flexibility of spirit in being willing to hear differing views and welcome new possibilities
4. Honors commitments and carries out personal promises

Thus an affirming approach—which applies equally to the parent-child relationship—reflects an attitude that is nondefensive (willing to admit mistakes), flexible (willing to hear differing views), and dependable (carries out promises).

Affirmation is a hopeful stance. As a mind-set, it conveys the conviction that every person is significant and has unique possibilities. A 1974 study found that what separates outstanding youth workers from the mediocre is not skill but an attitude of faith in their ability to change others.[2]

How can we affirm our adolescent child? A closer look at the seven goals for adolescents will show how parents may affirm their child in meaningful ways.

Goal 1—Achievement

Adolescents have a need to achieve, to excel in a tangible way (for example, in skills such as computer programming, playing football, sewing, painting, being a good mechanic). To know one does well in an activity vastly enhances one's sense of self-esteem.

The parent's task is to help the adolescent discover his or her "special gift" and then affirm each hesitant effort to develop this ability. The most devastating action of a parent is to fault, criticize, or demean the fumbling efforts of a child. In 1918 Charles Cooley said, "Pygmalion is alive and well in work with young people. Adults who convey a sense of futility to youth always seem to find their prophecy fulfilled, whereas those with great expectations likewise discover great potential in youth."[3] This is as true today as it was half a century ago.

Why should the parent not criticize the efforts of a child? Because the child's desperate short-term need is to gain a sense of achievement, to be seen as praiseworthy *now*. An adolescent needs affirmation and encouragement, not well-meaning criticism. An accurate critique can follow later.

An adolescent's need for parental praise and support can never be overestimated. Telling a child specific ways in which he or she has done well shows the adolescent that a parent has taken time to observe what he or she has done. Withholding affirmation or encouragement is often interpreted by children as an indication of parental lack of interest or even rejection. A friend recalls, "I can't remember ever getting a compliment as a teenager. I think my parents were afraid it would make me proud. But never knowing I did anything well made me feel like a nobody."

The opposite of this position, of course, is routine praise. "Don't praise every little thing," says a mother. "Kids can sort out what is phony or not. They also know what they can do well." If an adolescent has not done a task he or she was asked to do, or has performed poorly, we show we care by finding out why things did not work out. In the process, we may discover that the reason lies in a sense of inadequacy.

There may be situations, however, in which too much praise is hurtful. One young adult says, "I feel that I was praised more than necessary for my ability in athletics as a young adolescent. I think I developed the belief that I was more gifted than I really was. It caused some false hopes and expectations, which meant a long struggle with a sense of failure later on."

The adolescent's long-range need for achievement is centered in doing something significant in life, in finding a satisfying occupation or vocation. The 8,165 young adolescents in the Adolescent-Parent study were given a list of twenty-four values and asked to rank them in importance for their lives. Four top values (after a "happy family life") emerged:

1. To get a good job when I am older.
2. To do something important with my life.
3. To do well in school.
4. To make my parents proud of me.

The first two values (getting a good job and doing something important) are seen as being more important by ninth-graders than fifth-graders, whereas the next two (doing well in school and making parents proud) are regarded more highly by fifth-graders than by ninth-graders. Nevertheless, among the twenty-four values that adolescents of this age consider important, the average rank for these four values is from number two to number five. Clearly, the desire to achieve is a strong motivation for young adolescents. This means they will appreciate whatever their parents do to affirm and guide their exploratory thinking about a vocation or personal future.

Vocational choice becomes an increasingly important discussion topic as an adolescent matures. Figure 1 indicates the high ranking that adolescents grades five through nine give to the value of "doing something important with my life."

The significance of youth's desire to "do well in something" is shown in the 1990 study, *The Troubled Journey*. It demonstrates that an achievement motivation coupled with educational aspiration powerfully predict youth who will say no to at-risk behavior. It is an important value parents can help their children cultivate.[4]

Talking about the child's future career may be a way by which parents can counter the marked decline of ninth-grade boys' desire to achieve at school. Though the interest of girls in doing well at school remains high for grades five through nine, it steadily declines for boys. It may be that some boys shift their interest to other types of achievement. In response to the item, "At school I try as hard as I can to do my best work," 39 percent of the ninth-grade boys answer "very often," as compared with 49 percent of ninth-grade girls.

Granting this difference in academic motivation, it is well to recognize that 69 percent of the boys and 81 percent of the girls in the Adolescent-Parent study still aspire to go on to college. Of these, 26 percent of the boys and 31 percent of the girls entertain ideas of training for a profession. This suggests that thoughts about advanced education are already well-entrenched in the minds of middle-school adolescents.

We can help our adolescents find a sense of significance, but not by controlling them. Our data show that parental overcontrol, no matter how well-intentioned, has a dulling effect on the eductional aspirations of adolescents. Even worse than this type of guidance is overcontrol motivated by the personal ambitions of the parent (this emotional dynamic was discussed in Chapter 2 under "Unmet Needs").

A father may wish very much that his son play football, but the son might rather play chess. Chess, not football, is what

Figure 1. Achievement: Value placed on "doing something important with my life."*

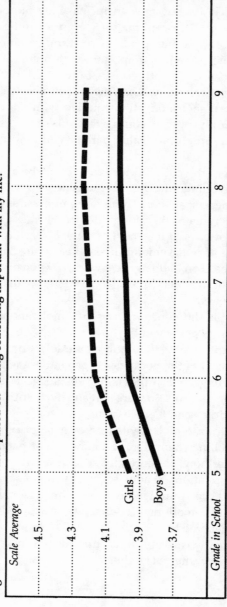

*5 = One of the 3 or 4 things I want most in life.
4 = I want this very much.
3 = I want this quite a bit.
2 = I want this somewhat.
1 = I don't want this much at all.

this boy needs to build confidence. A high school teacher expresses the problem:

I've been a high school drama and English teacher for five years now. My students have won top state awards in drama for the past three years. But my father feels I'm a failure because I'm not doing my medical residency at the Mayo Clinic.

The developmental goal of achievement is especially important for physically disabled adolescents. Though handicapped by cerebral palsy, Tom Janvier, while training for the Olympics, was asked, "What made the difference in your life?" Upon reflection, he decided that the more appropriate question would be, "*Who* made the difference?" Then he spoke of his parents as compassionate people who did not cease in their devotion to help him gain control over his uncontrollable muscles. In a speech entitled "I Don't Believe in Handicaps," he referred to his sisters, who loved him for himself; and to his speech teacher, who helped him share his feelings. These people helped him decide to be a winner when the odds against him were monumental.[5]

Goal 2—Friends

A second important goal for an emerging adolescent is gaining "friends I can count on." When asked about their interest in "learning how to make friends and be a friend," 52 percent of the boys and 69 percent of the girls in the Adolescent-Parent study say they "very much" wanted help in doing this. Why do they have this strong interest? Gaining friends is the adolescent's unconscious way of broadening his or her social base. In this way they can become integrated into a larger group without breaking from their parents.

Our task as parents is to affirm the adolescent's desire for friends and to open our home to these friends, thereby encouraging a broadening of the adolescent's social network. Peer friendships are extremely important. They help adolescents gain the skills needed for establishing lifelong friendships.

With increased skill in interpersonal relationships comes the ability to meet strangers, to feel comfortable in a group, and to be personally affirming of others. Unfortunately, in the 1970 Search Institute study of high school youth, we found that controlling parents show little interest in their child's friends, or, worse, are likely to disapprove of them. They actually discourage the widening of their child's friendship circle.

Boy-Girl Differences. As shown in Figure 2, marked differences do appear between the sexes on the goal of having friends. Girls are more concerned than boys about establishing friendships, a concern that for them does not change significantly by grade. Boys, who are less concerned about friends, also show less skill in interpersonal relationships.

Though parents notice the increase in their daughters' ability to relate well to people and to make friends, parents of boys do not see this improvement. As a result of having fewer social skills, boys do not cope as well in combating feelings of loneliness, being misunderstood, or being ridiculed. Clearly, social competence—the ability to make friends—is an important goal that tends to be underdeveloped among young adolescent boys. Skill in interpersonal relationships is at its highest for an adolescent boy when he is in seventh grade.

In contrast, ninth-grade girls are at their highest point in interpersonal relationships and lowest in their feelings of social alienation. It would appear that parents might enjoy a more comfortable relationship with their ninth-grade daughter than they may have had in her earlier stages of adolescence.

Parental Support. The adolescent's goal of gaining friends may be a turbulent road, as many parents know. A long-time teacher notes how prominently cliques figure in the lives of her fifth-graders. "The cliques sometimes change within a few weeks," she said. "And one thing I've noticed is the cruelty of some girls within a clique toward another. But the picked-on girl will stay because she wants to be a part of the friendship circle."

Parents may help make these friendship circles positive ex-

Figure 2. Friends: Value placed on friendship*

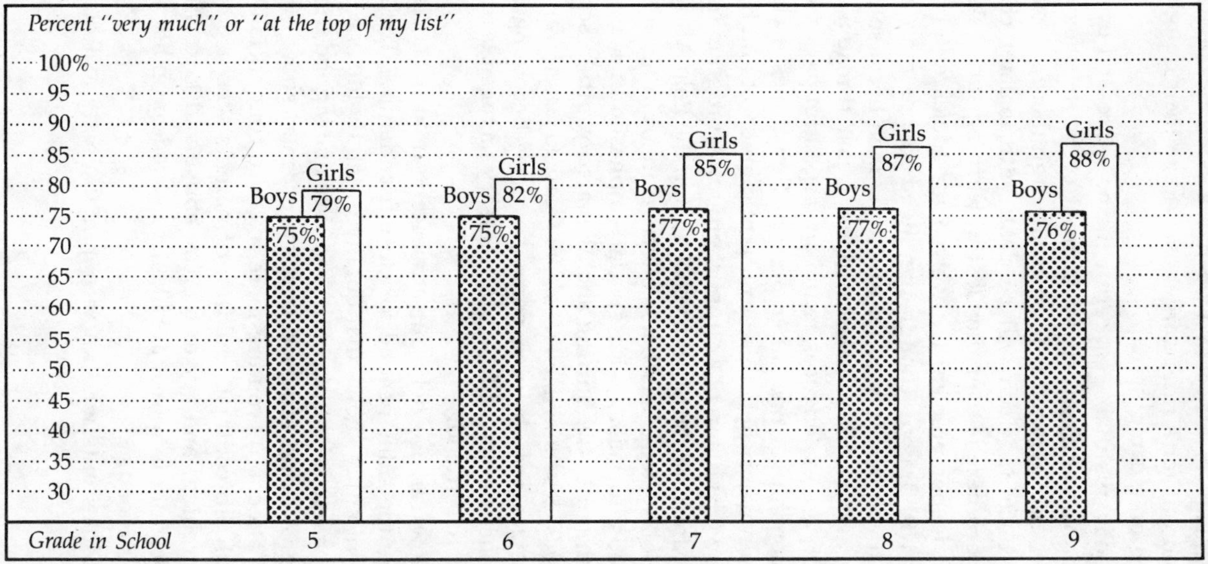

Percent "very much" or "at the top of my list"

	5	6	7	8	9
Girls	79%	82%	85%	87%	88%
Boys	75%	75%	77%	77%	76%

Grade in School

Item: How much do you want "to have friends you can count on"?

periences by providing fun occasions for friends to be together. For instance, a parent who has a boat may invite his son's friend out for a ride; parents may take their daughter's friend along on a camping trip.

Today, justifiable concern is being expressed over the hours an adolescent may spend in front of the television, the computer, or playing video games. Though there are other reasons for concern, which will be dealt with in later chapters, our concern here is over time lost in learning social skills.

A deeper problem is involved for adolescents who are shy and withdrawn. Though they need friends more than others do, they make it hard for this to happen because they tend to stay away from social situations. Least threatening for such youth are experiences found in large groups, or in the companionship of one other person. Sometimes a church youth leader may supply this important ingredient and be the bridge to the friendship of a support group. A program originated by Barbara Varenhorst, a psychologist in the Palo Alto, California, school system, has been effective in training adolescents in friendship skills, with special emphasis on learning how to reach out to the hurting and alienated youth in school. In *Real Friends: Becoming the Friend You'd Like to Have*,[6] Varenhorst emphasizes that helping someone else—becoming involved in another person's life—is a necessary factor in learning how to be a real friend.

How can we help our adolescents mature socially and acquire the skills needed for close friendships? The Adolescent-Parent study shows that quality of family life is a distinguishing characteristic of youth who have many good friends. Wherever you find family closeness (parental show of love, trust, and affection), you are more likely to find socially competent youth. In contrast, children of parents who are overly strict, controlling, and apt to employ abuse and love withdrawal as a form of discipline, are likely to have less ability to make and keep friends.

Adolescents who know parental abuse, feel hostile toward

their parents, and are involved in antisocial behavior tend to have few, if any, friends. Such characteristics are also associated with drug use and suicidal tendencies, even for adolescents as young as ten years old.

The Adolescent-Parent study strongly indicates that the adolescents who are apt to make friends easily are those most certain of a personal religious faith. They are also likely to see religion as liberating, rather than as a restrictive force that hems a person in with "do's" and "don't's." Clearly, participation in the life of a religious institution helps adolescents achieve this second developmental goal of making and keeping friends. They learn to become part of a larger family in which friendships are established on the basis of a common faith and shared values.

Goal 3—Feelings Understood

Learning how to share personal feelings with a trusted friend means learning to describe one's emotions in words. Doing so makes it possible for an adolescent to deal rationally with puzzling emotions.

The importance of this third goal became apparent to the research staff at Search Institute during a youth survey in 1959. Using a questionnaire that presented the range of youth concerns, respondents read each description and then indicated how much each item bothered them. After finishing the survey, young people often stayed around to talk. One remarked, "I enjoyed taking the survey because the items describe how I really feel. Not until I saw the words did I know what some of my feelings were."

We have discovered that the inability to describe feelings is a child's major block to communication with parents. Though they might want to discuss problems with a parent, some adolescents simply cannot. They feel inadequate to find words that express how they feel. All they can do is make a few unsuccessful attempts and then walk away, saying, "You just don't understand."

Here is where an adolescent's peer group plays an important role. In the nonthreatening setting of their own age group, adolescents explore their feelings. They fumble for words that describe their anxiety-producing experiences, and hear others do the same. This sharing of secrets and emotion-laden experiences helps adolescents develop the ability to share themselves. In this process the seemingly interminable phone conversations between teenagers, which are such an irritant to parents, are ways in which adolescents learn to verbalize feelings and share them with peers; entrusting themselves to another in this way, they gain the capacity to express affection and love. This can also be a positive outcome of friendships between boys and girls at this stage of development.

The value of friends in achieving the goal of sharing feelings is apparent. Increasingly, as adolescents grow older, they also desire help from their peers in coping with concerns. The number of youth who want such help increases steadily by grade in school.

As parents, our task in all this is to affirm and encourage our adolescent's stumbling efforts at describing inner thoughts and feelings. It is important to take time to listen carefully. A good "listening posture" on the part of the parent, described later in this chapter, is vital in helping children learn to share their feelings with others.

Adolescents who have not developed this ability say, "I can't talk about personal things with my friends," "It is hard for me to understand what other people are feeling," "It is hard for me to share my feelings with other people." In contrast, adolescents who have learned to share themselves will often say, "I know what my best friend is feeling before he or she even tells me."

Growth in coming close to another person includes growth in "feeling with" and understanding. It brings a sensitivity that is vital if one is to become a caring person. By the ninth grade, as indicated in Figure 3, girls are well ahead of boys in this ability. As though to compensate, boys seem to prefer

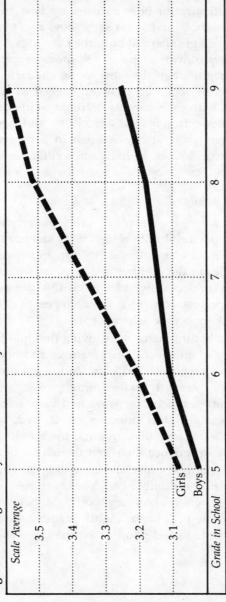

Figure 3. Feelings: Ability to establish intimacy*

Scale Average

3.5

3.4

3.3

3.2

3.1

Girls

Boys

Grade in School   5   6   7   8   9

Item: "It is easy for me to share my feelings with other people."
*Score is the average of 4 similar items.

5 = Very true
4 = Quite true
3 = Somewhat true
2 = A little true
1 = Not at all true

moving in cliques or gangs that serve to increase their sense of independence.

An obvious difficulty for boys in learning how to express emotion is the "macho" image that says "boys don't cry." This public image encourages them to bury their feelings and tough it out. That is why conversations to help boys verbalize their feelings should begin when they are young children. By fifth grade, or even before, children show an eagerness to discuss adolescent issues with their parents. Parents would do well to enter this open door. It is also at age eleven and twelve that adolescent children show strong interest in a personal God and concern for world need. Helping one's child verbalize his or her feelings on these subjects is a worthy goal for parents.

Goal 4—Identity Achieved

A big question for young people entering puberty is, "Who am I?" Dramatic portrayal of this search for identity is shown in Figure 4, which illustrates the sharp upturn between sixth and seventh grades in the number of adolescents who "spend a lot of time thinking about who I am." If this preoccupation with self is surprising, consider the changes that force an adolescent to look for a new self-concept.

First, enormous bodily changes are giving the child the physical characteristics of an adult. Facial features and body shape are beginning to change markedly, while the voice deepens, especially in boys. Strength and stamina increase, and with this comes a greater capacity for work and play. In boys, the growth of the testes and scrotum is accelerated, and they experience their first ejaculation. In girls, the breasts begin to develop, and they experience their first menstrual period.

These physical changes, especially unsettling for girls, cause a sharp increase in the number of adolescents who say "no" to the item "I feel good about my body." A negative trend among girls from the fifth to the eighth grades indicates how difficult it is for girls to feel good about the changes they are experiencing.

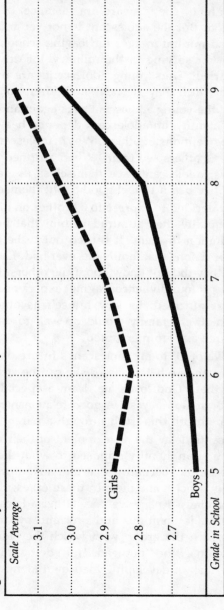

Figure 4. Identity: Concern about one's identity*

Scale Average

3.1
3.0
2.9
2.8
2.7

Girls

Boys

Grade in School

5   6   7   8   9

*Item: "I spend a lot of time thinking about who I am."
5 = Very true
4 = Quite true
3 = Somewhat true
2 = A little true
1 = Not at all true

A second major change that occurs relates to the role of the adolescent in society. An adolescent now is aware of leaving the child stage; he or she is aware, for instance, of drives for sexual expression. But the adolescent is not yet an adult. Society has defined minimum ages for leaving school, for being hired for a job, for serving in the military, for driving a car, for getting married. Thus young adolescents are in a transitional period in which they are neither children nor adults.

"Who am I?" the young adolescent asks again and again. In this search for identity, an adolescent depends heavily on the reactions and perceptions of others. Why? Adolescents tend to see themselves as others see them. When affirmed as significant individuals, adolescents see themselves as people who are respected; they begin to feel good about themselves.

Irene's family decided to express to a brother on his birthday some positive quality they admired in him that had been a source of inspiration to them. It turned out to be one of the most intimate occasions that family has ever had. Each of them learned things they did not know about the others. More than that, it was a profoundly encouraging experience for their brother. He was affirmed; he saw himself as others in the family saw him. Every family would do well to do this in a setting that is free and uninterrupted.

Most pervasive of all to an adolescent's future development and sense of worth is whether he or she can be strengthened in the concept that "God loves me. I am a special person. I have great worth in God's eyes." A good relationship is needed if the child is to absorb this truth through a parent.

Some adolescents delay the development of their own sense of self by adopting an identity opposed to what their parents stand for (for example, becoming a sexual adventurer in reaction to an overly strict home life). In these cases, the identity adopted is essentially a negative one. Other adolescents may slip into ready-made identities and proclaim by dress, mannerism, and speech the group with which they identify (the "jocks," the "brains," the "potheads"). In doing this, they are postponing the task of developing their own identity.

Adolescents who willingly identify with their families achieve positive self-identity more easily. The child who can find satisfaction and pride in knowing he or she is the son or daughter of the O'Briens, or the Johnsons, or the Taylors, can more quickly come to an awareness of who he or she is. But for children who have had several fathers or mothers in the course of growing up, identifying with a family name is less possible. For some adolescents, the resultant feelings of separateness and aloneness makes the goal of self-identity more difficult to achieve.

Slow developers (usually boys), for whom puberty is delayed until as late as the ninth grade, also have their problems. Small and undeveloped physically, they are easily shunted aside. Granted the status of neither children nor adults, they also are not viewed as adolescents. Those who mature late feel the impact of this nonidentity socially and personality-wise; they especially need the emotional support of parents and friends. Parents must help them understand that the "internal clock" may vary considerably from person to person.

Goal 5—Responsibility Accepted

One day, while we were seated in a restaurant in western Colorado, someone drew our attention to a nest of blue swallows outside the window. The fledgling birds were peering over the edge of the nest to the cement walk eight feet below. The mother bird, having decided it was time for her four offspring to try their wings, was nudging them ever closer to the edge of the nest. It was fascinating to witness the reluctance of these fledglings to leave their nest, and the insistence of the mother that they start flying.

The analogy of a bird nudging her offspring out of the nest is apt. While we tend to think that youth's drive for independence is rooted in rebelliousness, the drive originates just as much with parents. We found this to be true in our study: Most parents want their children to begin accepting adult responsibilities and making decisions on their own. Most parents want their children to leave home as self-reliant, responsible adults. Carrying out this conviction, however, is not easy. Many parents are afraid of how their adolescent will abuse this freedom. As a result, parents tend to shelter their growing adolescents and act in ways that make them unable to take independent actions.

The Adolescent-Parent study shows that youth-parent conflict is not a major issue during the junior high school years. Nor does conflict occur more for boys than for girls, nor does youth-parent conflict increase significantly from grades five through nine. What does change over the years, however, is the number of adolescents who want to "make my own decisions." Without question, there is a growing desire for independence during this stage in life. Figure 5 shows the rise in need for autonomy between the fifth and ninth grades, a change from 43 percent in fifth grade to 63 percent in ninth grade.

Clearly, the fifth goal for a maturing adolescent is to become behaviorally independent. Who achieves this goal best? Interestingly, it is those adolescents who view their parents with respect and affection. Although parents will note a greater resistance to authority as their adolescent moves toward ninth grade and, hence, occasions when sparks will fly, the increase in hostility is minimal. The change is primarily in an adolescent's reaction to parental roles.

The parent's task in helping an adolescent to accept responsibility is to avoid a smothering, rule-oriented, overcontrolling approach that keeps a child dependent on the parent or forces a rebellious response that results in rash and hurtful decisions.

The parent's task is to involve the adolescent in the basics of decision making, which should ideally begin in early childhood. Two young adults, when asked what ingredients they would consider essential in the homes they hope to establish, give some helpful insights into this process. One says,

I would teach responsibility, not by leading my child by the hand and telling him/her what should be done, but by teaching my child to think and make independent decisions. I would help him/her practice by creating a thinking situation, and then taking time to explain what

Figure 5. Responsibility: Desire to make own decisions*

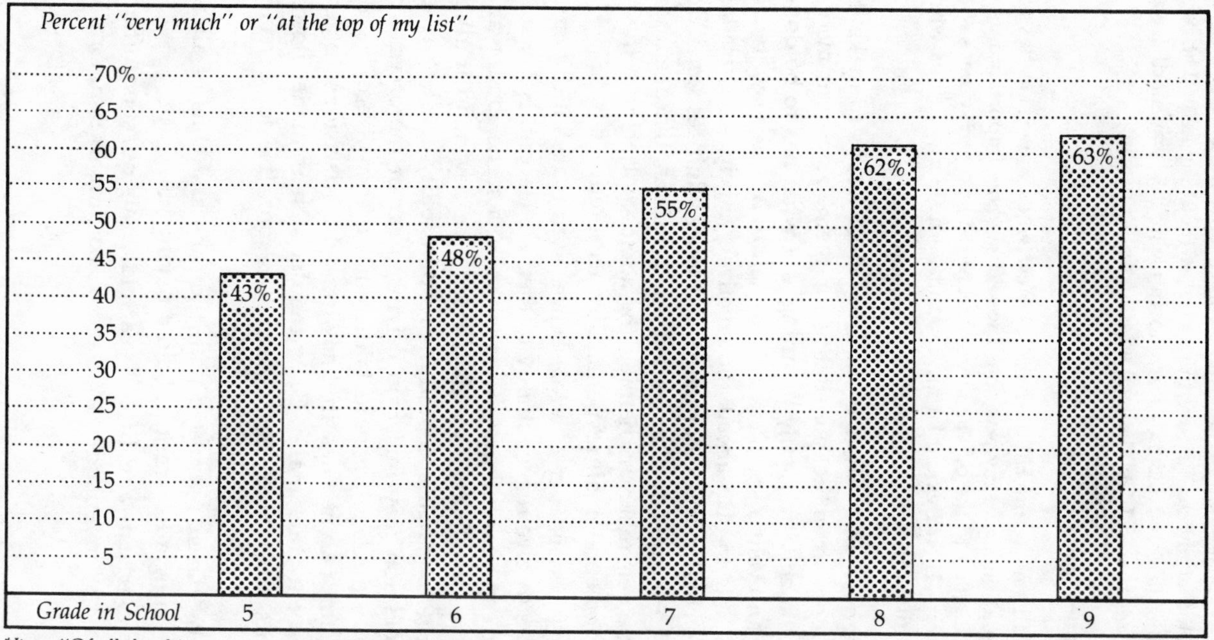

Percent "very much" or "at the top of my list"
70%
65
60
55
50
45
40
35
30
25
20
15
10
5
43%
48%
55%
62%
63%
Grade in School
5
6
7
8
9

*Item: "Of all the things you want in life, how much do you want to make your own decisions?"

I, as a parent on the basis of my experience, think are important things to consider and what are not, in making the decision. I would then ask that my child figure things out without my help. The reason I say this is that I did not learn to think in this way until I was a young adult, and I feel the lack was hurtful to me.

The other adds,

I would listen to my child's point of view when a decision has to be made and then give my position. I would say how important it is that we each listen to the other's ideas, sort of get into each other's shoes, as it were. Then I would let my child make his/her decisions without my butting in.

Taught in this way, the maturing child learns to make decisions and accept responsibility for them. A parent also can involve a child in family planning and what has to be done to make an event a satisfactory experience. In this way, the child learns how to plan ahead and creatively anticipate future tasks. As the child grows older, more and more adult responsibilities may be assumed. The parent who affirms these efforts to become self-reliant is helping the adolescent achieve the fifth developmental goal: responsibility accepted.

The inconsistency of adolescence often makes it difficult for parents to give responsibility to their adolescent. For example, a fourteen-year-old daughter may make a scene about wanting more responsibility; two days later, she may hand it all back or forget she had accepted the responsibility at all. A fifteen-year-old son may insist on driving a car or motorcycle, oblivious to the legal responsibilities that are involved. The difficulty for parents lies in knowing what decisions to let an adolescent child make. Once the decision is made, however, parents must hold the adolescent responsible for carrying it out.

Many parents struggle with the pros and cons of allowing their young adolescent to hold a paying job.

For fourteen- and fifteen-year-olds, this question often becomes an "independence" issue. According to Simmons Market Research Bureau,[7] three in five teenagers between fifteen and seventeen years of age and one in two twelve- to fourteen-year-olds are employed.

One positive aspect of teenage employment is that they learn to assume responsibility and help the family financially. One might also expect that the adolescent would learn the value of a dollar. This is not necessarily so, however; the University of Michigan's Institute for Social Research found that most of the high school seniors it surveyed used most or all of their earnings for immediate pleasure.[8]

Fifteen-year-olds who work more than fifteen hours a week on the average do less well in school and are less involved in school activities than those who do not work. Teens who have jobs, according to a study done at the University of California at Irvine, "tend to use cigarettes, alcohol, marijuana, and other drugs more often than unemployed adolescents, partly because they have more available cash and partly because they are subjected to more stress."[9]

A parent who gives an adolescent permission to get a job needs to help the child make the work experience a positive step in reaching maturity. This means considering such possibilities as taking a job that offers opportunities for learning; limiting the number of work hours so there is time for school and church activities on weekday evenings and Sundays; and encouraging long-term goals, such as saving for a college education. It could be a worthwhile experience for parent and adolescent to work out guidelines together, and have checkpoint times to see how the goals are being met. The end result could be progress toward the goal of achieving a sense of responsibility.

When parents talk of adolescents' accepting responsibility, they are often thinking of doing dishes, mowing the lawn, shoveling snow, cleaning the room, not as work for which they receive pay, but which is done as a member of the family. Other aspects of responsibility are overlooked. A young person grows in maturity by accepting responsibility for making an ill or unhappy family member feel better; or by accepting responsibility for reconciling family differences. This does not mean assuming the role of "the responsible one," but giving opportunities for each person in the family to struggle to a point of maturity. Of course, parents need to be aware of each adolescent's different abilities and not expect the impossible. Part of wisdom is expecting decision making only in areas where the adolescent is equipped to do it. Affirming a child's acceptance of responsibility is important.

Goal 6—Maturity

The end goal of all the developmental tasks, of course, is maturity—the state of having been transformed from a child to an adult. Though the onset of adolescence begins with a sharp break from childhood, the end of adolescence is not as clearly defined. Some adults never do complete their developmental tasks. They live as immature people whose behaviors are often quite adolescent.

Sexual maturity is another dimension of growing up. We asked the 10,467 parents of young adolescents to describe their child in relation to puberty. One question was, "To what extent has your child gone through puberty—that is, the period of time when the body takes on adult characteristics (for example, body hair grows, girls' breasts develop, boys' voices deepen). Which of the following is truest for your child?"

1. My child has not yet begun to go through puberty.
2. My child is in the beginning of puberty.
3. My child is in the middle of puberty.
4. My child is almost through puberty.
5. My child has completely gone through puberty.

Table 2. Parents' Estimates of Child's Reaction to Puberty

Grade in school	Boys					Girls				
	5	6	7	8	9	5	6	7	8	9
A. % Not yet begun puberty	86%	65%	38%	15%	5%	33%	14%	5%	1%	1%
B. % Beginning puberty	14	31	48	44	18	58	56	42	18	6
C. % In middle of puberty	0	3	11	26	41	7	22	31	31	21
D. % Almost through puberty	0	1	3	13	29	2	5	13	29	35
E. % Completed puberty	0	0	0	3	7	1	3	9	20	37

Note the growth trend in pubertal development indicated in Table 2. Two-thirds of the parents of girls believe their fifth-grader has entered puberty, and only fifteen percent of the parents of boys. Notice that the onset of puberty has not begun for some boys in eighth or ninth grade. There is a variability among young adolescents of at least five years. Interestingly, a few parents of girls think their child has completed puberty by the fifth or sixth grade (ages eleven and twelve), whereas over a third feel it did not happen until ninth grade (age fifteen). It is possible that parents themselves are not sure what constitutes entering or completing puberty.

Probably the most important fact to note is that girls mature sexually about two years earlier than boys. The average age at onset of menstruation is thirteen years; the average age at first ejaculation of semen is fifteen. See Figure 6.

Goal 7—Sexuality Understood

As already noted, a major component in the onset of adolescence is growth toward sexual maturity. This goal for an adolescent is acceptance of the new role of being a potential mother or father and acceptance of the responsibility sexual maturity implies. The task for the parent is to affirm the adolescent in this development and help him or her understand what is taking place.

The increased sex drive that accompanies onset of puberty is shown in the rising percentage of young adolescents who are interested in the opposite sex, as shown in Figure 7. The percentage who think "often" or "very often" about sex increases each year, from 24 percent for fifth-grade boys to 50

Figure 6. Maturity: Pubertal development by grade*

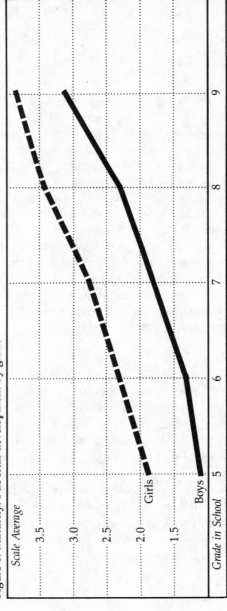

*5 = My child has *completely* gone through puberty
4 = My child is *almost* through puberty
3 = My child is *in the middle* of puberty
2 = My child is *beginning* to go through puberty
1 = My child has *not yet begun* to go through puberty

percent for ninth-grade boys. Though two years behind girls in their physical development, boys do not lag in the number who think often about sex. They respond more readily to sexual stimuli when alone, in contrast to girls, who respond more readily to affectional stimuli.

With thoughts of sex come an increased percentage who frequently talk about it. The number who talk "often" or "very much" with their friends about sex steadily increases from 26 percent (fifth grade) to 48 percent (ninth grade). It is a topic that new drives and emotions make exciting and daring. For many, talk about sex becomes a way of coming to understand and accept this new phenomenon in their lives.

A parent should know that the likelihood of an adolescent adopting a responsible attitude to sexuality is influenced by a variety of forces. The Adolescent-Parent data show that adolescents raised in families characterized by nurturance, warmth, and cohesiveness are significantly less likely to become attracted to sexually arousing stimuli or to become involved in sexual activity. The same is true for adolescents who view religion as important in their lives or who are raised by devout parents.

The adolescents who find it most difficult to accept a responsible approach to sexuality are those who as children have suffered sexual abuse. The tragic impact is the tendency of an abused child to repeat the cycle when he or she is older. For some reason not readily apparent to us, girls in the fifth grade are more likely (compared to girls in grades six through nine) to be afraid of sexual coercion.

Significantly, sexuality is a dimension of life adolescents wish they could discuss with their parents. When asked to indicate the one "to whom they most likely would turn for help or advice when having questions about sex," their overwhelming preference was parents. Though the percentage that prefer parents drops sharply following the seventh grade, there are still more ninth-graders who prefer their parents to personal friends or other adults for help or advice.

Figure 7. Sexuality: Frequency of Thinking About Sex*

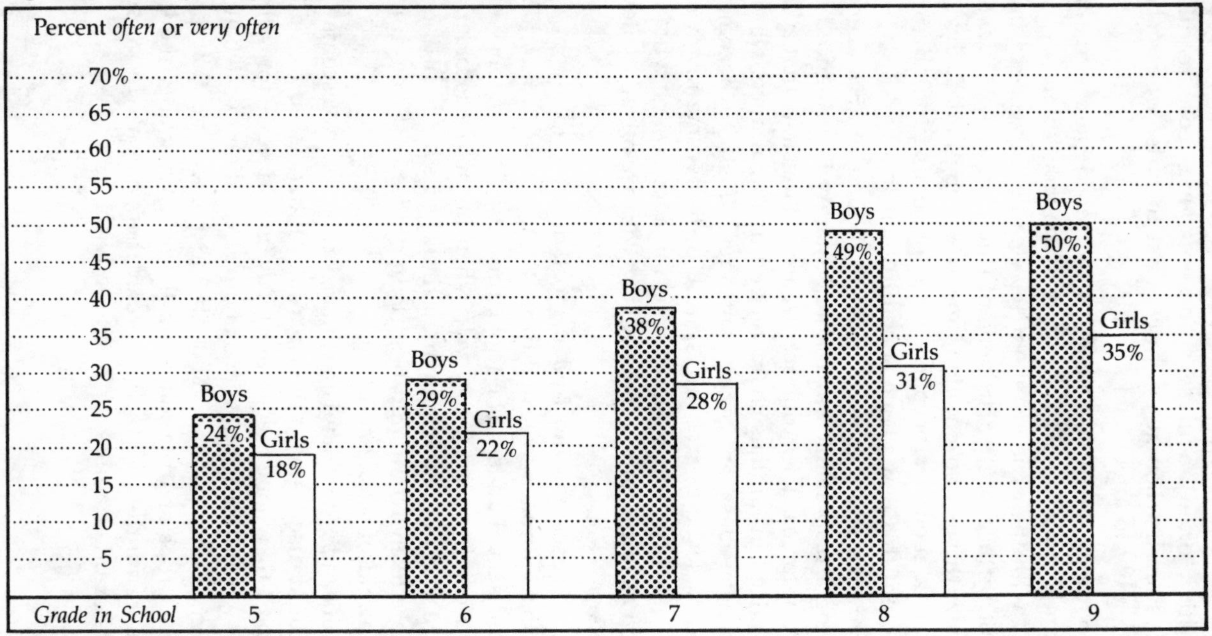

Percent *often* or *very often*

Grade in School

Item: "How often do you think about sex?"

Clearly, the time of opportunity for helping adolescents understand and responsibly accept their potential for creating life is in these early adolescent years. Unfortunately, most parents fail to take advantage of this opportunity. Only one-third of the adolescents in the Adolescent-Parent study say that they "have had good talks with my parents about sex." Yet, for half the young adolescents in grades six through nine, it is an especially pertinent topic of conversation. Fifty percent say they are "in love with someone of the opposite sex." The task of a parent is to affirm the significance of boy-girl attraction, a God-created phenomenon, and help the adolescent understand its meaning and beauty. Parents are most helpful to their adolescent sons and daughters when they can discuss not only the facts of sex, but the emotions and responsibilities involved. Parents need to evaluate their own feelings on sex issues in order to be the help they want to be to their adolescent.

A girl speaking about her mother's relationship to her in the matter of sex conversation says,

I'd like to talk to my mom more openly about my boyfriend, especially how to handle sexual desires so I can stay in keeping with God's Word. She doesn't have time for me. Or, when she does, I feel like she's not really understanding. I'm embarrassed to talk openly to her because I feel like she won't approve or accept my feelings. So, I feel like I always have to be my best. It doesn't give me any room to deal with my humanness and faults and to know that I'm loved.[10]

The conceptual framework for understanding early adolescence presented earlier can be helpful to us as parents if we use it to organize what we hear and observe in our children. It is important to allow conversation to go below the surface of routine exchange. To have such conversations we must sit down and listen with an attitude of truly wanting to understand our child. The following section discusses how this stance of understanding can be established.

Listening for Understanding

"Of course I know more than a child. . . ."

Adults typically think they know more than children. From such a vantage point, we relate to our children much as doctors relate to their patients. We ask questions (often probing ones) to locate trouble spots. Having heard the answers and made a judgment, we give a prescription as to what should be done. From our position of authority, we expect our prescription to be followed.

From this stance also, we may relate to our child as a teacher does to a student. We feel free to correct a mistake, or to give information. This may be a helpful way to operate with small children, but we need additional skills with adolescents. Because they are entering into adulthood, they will respond better to being approached as peers. Essentially, the path to such understanding is a *listening stance.*

Three Types of Listening Mistakes

The concept of a listening stance is well known. In fact, most of the parents in our study say they often listen to their adolescent. Unfortunately, however, listening is not easily practiced. Roland and Doris Larson, in *I Need to Have You Know Me,* describe common "listening mistakes" of well-meaning people.[11] These mistakes illustrate that the kind of listening most busy people do does not represent the "listening from the heart" that adolescents need.

Listening with Half an Ear. This is a common form of listening within a family setting. Let us imagine a scene wherein thirteen-year-old Barb storms into the house in angry tears. It seems that her best friend, Cindy, has broken a trust. Barb told her a personal secret and made Cindy promise she would tell no one. But Cindy did tell someone, and Barb is furious. "I hate her!" she cries. "I never want to see her again!"

Barb's mother is busy. It's only a few minutes before supper and she is making a tossed salad and keeping an eye on the roast in the oven. She is sympathetic, though, and asks a few questions. But then she says briskly, "Just a minute, Barb. I have to check on the meat." She turns away and opens the oven door. "Oh, dear, it's getting overdone! Keep talking, Barb; I can hear you." Barb does try to continue, but somehow it's not as easy to talk when someone isn't looking at you and is preoccupied with something else.

The mother faces Barb again. "Now, as you were saying about Cindy. . . ." Barb's face brightens and conversation picks up. Then suddenly the mother interrupts again. "Oh, oh, I forgot to put the broccoli on and your father will be home any minute. I'll be right back." She runs downstairs to the freezer. What has happened when she returns? Barb has gone up to her room. The mother has missed a chance to enter into a painful experience with her daughter. Moreover, this is the age when a friend's betrayal is crushing. Talking about it could have brought insight into the situation; it could have brought healing.

What can a parent do in a situation such as this? After all, the mother was legitimately busy. But if one is going to listen, one has to stop what one is doing and tune in to the other person's feelings. If possible, even at a busy time such as before supper, the mother needs to listen intently for a few minutes and then explain that this is a difficult time to talk. She and her daughter should then agree to have further conversation as soon as possible. The most important element is that the adolescent knows she is being heard. Her problem is important enough to warrant her mother's time later, if not right now. Self-worth is preserved.

"Yes, But" Listening. Let us imagine the same scene between Barb and her mother. This time the mother is attentive. She hears the story, asks a few questions, then quickly launches into her "advice" treatment.

"But Barb, don't you remember I told you that if you ever want anything broadcast all over town, tell Cindy? Her mother is just like her? There are some things you're going to have to learn in life, Barb. You're too trusting—just like your father. I don't mean you should be suspicious of everyone, but you have to be smart about things like that. . . ."

Barb has already left the room. Anger at Cindy is now mingled with anger at her mother. Reinforced inside her is the conviction, all too common for adolescents, that you can't tell grown-ups anything. They just scold you and tell you what you *should* have done.

There is a strong possibility that Barb's mother gave sound advice. After all, she has lived longer than Barb, knows her community and, no doubt, more about human nature. But she didn't give the gift of herself in listening; she merely gave advice. And she missed the opportunity to help Barb discover her own way of dealing positively with this painful experience.

"I Can Top That" Listening.   In this instance, Barb's mother hears part of the story. Then she says, "That's tough, Barb, but you'll get over it. If you think this is bad, let me tell you what happened when I was your age—well, maybe a year older—I can't remember exactly what year it was. But I remember I lived at the house on 32nd Street. Anyway . . . " the mother is now very animated, thinking of the incident in her past " . . . I had a friend named Joyce. We were really close. I told her that I had a crush on a boy in our class and I swore her to secrecy and she promised. The next day when I came to biology class it was plastered all over the blackboard, 'Annie loves Jack'—Jack was the boy's name . . . "

The mother looks at Barb, whose face bears little expression. In fact, she is putting on her coat, ready to leave.

What has happened? The mother has taken all the limelight, shifted the attention to herself. She never entered into her daughter's problem.

A young man remembers:

My warmest feeling about home was coming back from school and talking to Mom, answering questions like, "What did you do today?" and "How did you feel about school today?" As I think about the family I might have in the future, I find myself wanting to give quality time listening to my children in a noncondemning way. I want to listen to *who they are* and how they feel.

As a mother, I remembered with fondness and gratitude the many long talks our sons and I had together in their growing-up years. One instance in particular comes to my mind now. When one of our sons was in seventh grade, he often would ask me to come into his bedroom after he had gone to bed just so we could talk. In that quiet, dark place, frustrations and dreams were listened to and shared, even though sometimes I was very tired and would rather have gone to bed myself. In eighth grade, he went through a turbulent, rebellious time. Not once during that time did he ask me to come in and talk at night. I never said anything about it, either. You can imagine what it meant to me when, at the beginning of ninth grade, he said one night, "Mom, can you come in and talk?"

How to Listen

Listening with the heart is a basic requirement for understanding our adolescent sons and daughters. It is the only way by which we as parents can come to understand the thoughts and concerns and feelings unique to adolescents. It is also the only way by which we as parents can come to understand that *person* who is our child, regardless of his or her age. Listening is a vital aspect of parenting. A careful empirical study, *Families of the Slums* by S. Minuchin and others, has documented that multiproblem families are groups of people who do not listen to one another. In those families there is no experience of making contact with each other, of counting as persons.[12]

In learning how to listen with the heart, consider the following insight from Barbara Varenhorst's book *Real Friends*:

Heart listening can be learned, but it cannot be practiced or done mechanically. You can listen mechanically with your ears, but not with your heart. Why? Because the essence of listening with your heart is to put your whole self into trying to hear what the other is saying, because you care that much. Unless you care, you won't stop talking, resisting, or ignoring long enough to hear what is being said. You won't sacrifice your time or convenience to hear the other's feelings behind the words or the twisted behaviors. If you care enough, you will learn the necessary skills, and then you will practice repeatedly, putting out the effort needed to learn to listen with your heart.[13]

Given below are three important guidelines for listening. These are not techniques you can pick up and use immediately as an instant solution. Rather, they represent an approach that must be learned and perfected over time. They shift the parent's approach away from being an authority figure to being that child's peer. The net effect is that the adolescent feels that he or she is being treated more like an adult. We have used these techniques ourselves, and have found them to be highly effective in our own family life.

Guide 1. Listen in Ways That Encourage Expression of Feelings.

Adolescence is a time of bewildering emotions and intense new feelings. This includes sexual desires, fantasies, grandiose ambitions, dreams, anger at being treated like a child, and strange feelings about bodily changes. Not until an adolescent *identifies these feelings with words* will he or she begin to handle them in a rational, mature way.

Years ago, in conducting five-day youth counseling seminars for pastors, we brought in young people to assist us in the training. For two separate evenings, the pastors sat and actively listened to these youth share their concerns (and later their evaluations of how well the pastors listened). We were impressed by the fact that many friendships were formed between the pastors and youth, friendships that often continued through the year via letters. When several youths were queried about these friendships, one said, "You don't understand. Never before in my life have I had an adult listen to me for forty-five minutes. It's a good experience." We came to realize there are few times an adolescent is able to speak freely to an adult without being stopped short by a reprimand or correction.

The first essential in listening is to convey an attitude of warm interest, free from a spirit of judgment or criticism. This cannot be faked. If a parent is unable honestly to adopt such a stance, it will be sensed. An adolescent is quick to judge a parent's attitude from the tone of voice, set of the lips, or facial expressions. A parent will be able to convey a nonjudgmental affirming attitude only if that is the attitude the parent has. Much of what is needed in a listening posture flows out of this attitude of warmth and unconditional regard.

A second essential in listening is to use two kinds of verbal responses, each of which tends to encourage conversation.

Affirming Responses. Adolescents, self-conscious because of their lack of skill in expressing themselves, appreciate comments that are accepting, approving, affirming. It is reassuring to the adolescent to hear a parent say, "I can understand what you're saying," or "I can appreciate your willingness to tell me that," or "Good! You're saying it well."

This type of affirming response can dispel fears adolescents have when talking about themselves with an authority figure: "Are my comments worth hearing? Do I make sense? Do I sound like a nut?" Once adolescents feel they are being heard and appreciated, their reaction is to talk more freely.

General Leads Instead of Specific Questions. Authority figures tend to use highly specific questions. These have the effect of placing an adolescent on the defensive or in a dependency role. Its observable effect is to reduce conversation to responses that become shorter and shorter.

Far better are "general leads" that give the adolescent freedom to share what he or she chooses. Some "general leads" might be: "Mind telling me about your game today?" or "Would you care to explain that more fully?" or "Could you give me a 'for instance'?"

These convey an open-endedness that allows an adolescent to share what he or she wishes. The net effect of this type of verbal response is to increase comments from the adolescent.

Guideline 2. Listen to Discern the Adolescent's Perspective.

This means listening to discern "where your adolescent is coming from." It means trying to understand how your child views life. It means trying to view a situation through the eyes of your adolescent.

It doesn't mean that at this point we stop being parents. But it does mean that we make a deliberate effort to know the inner life and feelings of our child. Such knowledge is a parent's best guide for determining how best to respond.

Listening to discern an adolescent's perspective is an active process that is helped by the use of two additional kinds of verbal responses. They are worth practicing because they are effective in helping one listen more sensitively and in establishing a close relationship.

Feedback Responses. It is helpful when a parent responds to an adolescent's comments by saying, "Let me tell you what I am hearing, to see if I am on target," or, "In other words, you. . . . Does that sound right?"

These responses convey the idea that you as an adult are trying to understand what is being said. All you are doing is using your own words to restate or summarize what the other person has just said. If you have heard correctly and stated it well, the adolescent's reaction will be to say, "That's right," and then continue telling his or her story. If you are not accurate in your feedback, you might hear, "No, that's not what I meant." Your response has given the child a chance to clarify what has been said.

Clarification Responses. Clarification means going further than just restating or summarizing what you have heard. It means trying to interpret what you hear. It involves listening for the feelings being expressed through words. It is listening with a third ear. You might indicate your interpretation of what you hear by comments such as these: "You resent Dad's absence from your games. Is that correct?" or, "You feel we're picking on you. Is that it?"

It does not matter that the clarifying response may be off-target. If you are not grasping what your child is saying, you have encouraged him or her to go into greater detail in explaining the situation. Adolescents feel complimented if a parent takes the time to hear them out while intently trying to understand.

The net effect of this kind of "listening from the heart" is a closer relationship between parent and adolescent.

Guideline 3. Approach Each Conversation with a Sense of Hope.

The adolescent may be fearful and deeply troubled. Trapped by peer pressure, he or she may have become involved in problems created by drug or alcohol abuse, sexual activity, vandalism. It is important that we as parents are able to reflect the conviction that there is hope, regardless of the situation.

This hope can be based on our faith in the child and the possibilities we see that can be unlocked. Adolescents sensing this confidence in them will receive it as "good news" of the highest order.

For some parents, this hope finds its ultimate source in the belief that God can change things and is seeking to do so for their child. This confidence in God gives a sense of hope to the conversations they have with their child.

4. Cry for a Close Family

If the family were a container, it would be a nest, an enduring nest, loosely woven, expansive, and open.

If the family were a fruit, it would be an orange, a circle of sections, held together but separable—each segment distinct.

—LETTY COTTIN POGREBIN

When they were children, there had been much togetherness in their family—long trips and weeks of camping. But as the years wore on, the closeness eroded. Father was frustrated because his children were not developing in the directions he would have chosen, and his reaction was interpreted by his adolescents as failure on their part. Because he didn't take time to develop a listening stance, Father missed chances to "read" his children. The "Yes, but . . . " response (see Chapter 3) often came too quickly in his conversations with his adolescent children.

Mother saw the gap widening, but her warnings went unheard. The family became fractured, and there was a distance of spirit between sons, daughters, and father. But Father was a caring man. Sensing things had gone awry, he began to create opportunities for the children to be with him individually and with the family as a group. Gradually, the old sense of camaraderie began to reappear; the grown children began to look forward to being together. Most of all, the children began to understand their father. . . .

This father's cry for the closeness that he and his family once knew exemplifies the theme of this chapter: the deep desire of parents and children alike to experience the happiness of a close family life. In the Adolescent-Parent study, both groups gave "a happy family" the highest rank of importance.

But the ideal of a "happy family life" is neither easy to

achieve nor to maintain. In evaluating *how well* members of their family "get along with each other," and *how true* it is that "there is a lot of love in our family," adolescents' and parents' combined ratings decline as the children grow older (see Figure 8).

Does this mean that ninth-graders are more disruptive and harder to handle than fifth-graders? No. Repeated measures show the opposite to be true: Parents report less difficulty in handling ninth-graders than fifth-graders. Why, then, the decline in family closeness? Because there is also a decline during these years in:

- Parental harmony
- Parent-youth communication
- Parental discipline or control
- Parental nurturing

These are four essential elements for a close family life. When present they serve as a source of strength for adolescents.

Parental Harmony

The relationship between husband and wife changes noticeably as their children grow older. Adolescents entering the ninth grade notice less exchange of affection (for example, hugging and kissing) between their parents, and they are aware that their parents argue more and get "mad at each other." When evaluating how well their parents "get along with each other," adolescents' rating decreases significantly from fifth-grade to ninth-grade.

Do the 10,467 parents in the study agree with their children's evaluation? Yes. When the parents rated the happiness of their marital relationship, the number who agreed that their relationship was "very" or "extremely" happy dropped from 67 percent for parents of fifth-grade youth to 61 percent among parents of ninth-graders. That difference, though a significant

Figure 8. Change in Family Closeness*

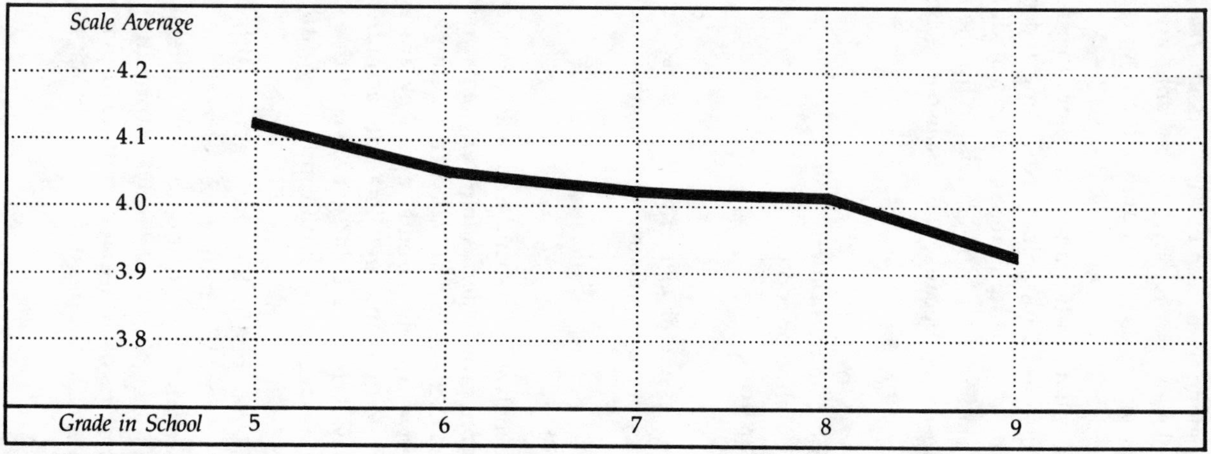

Item: "Members of my family get along well with each other."

*Based on the average of 4 items

5 = Almost always true
4 = Often true
3 = Sometimes true
2 = True once in a while
1 = Never true

drop, is not a great one. Probably more important is the fact that one in five of the 10,467 parents admitted that their marital relationship is not happy. One in two report times of arguing or "getting mad at" each other. Of these, one in eight says it happens "often" or "very often."

We also asked several specific questions in the survey about how adult partners handle their disagreements or arguments. Two out of three mothers acknowledge times when they were given the "silent treatment." One out of four mothers said that there were at least six times during the year when a partner "raised his voice, insulted me, or swore at me."

One in five remember times in the past year when a husband threw, smashed, kicked, or hit something in the home. One in ten mothers admit to having been pushed, shoved, or grabbed; and a few report having been hit (7 percent) or beaten up (2 percent).

These occasions illustrate what sociologists David Olson and Hamilton McCubbin call the "storm and stress" stage in the family life cycle.[2] Pressures on parents are such that during the children's adolescent years, parental harmony drops to its lowest point.

In Chapter 2 we discussed parental stresses under the topic "Understanding Yourself as a Parent." There we identified emotional forces and types of stressful circumstances that can cause parental disharmony and encourage a strained, cold, or embattled relationship. When parents don't get along, it causes real distress for adolescents. In *Five Cries of Youth*, we reported that almost 60 percent of the youth who feel like psychological orphans in their home (due to parental disharmony) sometimes consider suicide.[3]

Even though parents may try to hide their conflict from the children, it is doubtful that they really succeed. In *The Family Crucible*[4] family therapist Augustus Napier says he frequently finds that the problems of a troublemaking child or adolescent can be traced to some strain in the husband-wife relationship that is upsetting the balance of family life. For instance, where there is parental conflict, a parent may begin to get needed affection from a child rather than the spouse. This shift may be a subtle one, but it shows that outside help may be necessary to gain the needed insights into what is happening within such a family structure.

In our 1971 survey of high school youth we pursued the issue of factors that predict family disunity. Through a complex analysis of the data, we found that one item outranks all other factors: "My father and mother do not get along with each other. This bothers me very much." *This simple statement is our most powerful indicator of family disharmony.* Where father and mother are at odds with each other, the whole family suffers. The children become psychological orphans.[5]

An added problem for children is the common but debilitating fear that they are to blame for their parents' fighting. For this reason, as well as for their own sakes, parents embroiled in conflict will do their children a favor by seeking outside counseling.

Family closeness actually fortifies children with an inner resistance to the toxins of life. The Adolescent-Parent study shows that adolescents in a close family unit are the ones most likely to say "no" to drug use, pre-marital sexual activity, and other antisocial and alienating behaviors. They are also the ones most likely to adopt high moral standards, develop the ability to make and keep friends, embrace a religious faith, and involve themselves in helping activities. All of these characteristics pertaining to adolescents from close families are significant—which means that the evidence cannot be attributed to mere chance.

Parent-Youth Communication

The importance of good parent-youth communication has been evident to us from the very beginning of the Adolescent-Parent study. When 2,000 youth filled in answers to item stems beginning "I wish . . . ", they often responded, "I wish

I could talk to my folks about some of my problems." The frequent response of 2,000 parents to the same item stem was, "I wish I could talk with my teenager about the things troubling him."

The responses point up the impasse in communication that both parents and adolescents wish could be broken. Some parents indicated specific areas in which they had poor communication with their children:

The hardest thing to talk to my child about is racial relationships and social standings.

The hardest thing to talk to my child about is what he should expect to encounter in the areas of drugs, sex, alcohol, and relationships with other people as he approaches adulthood.

The hardest thing to talk to my children about is their father's drinking behavior and the time he and I spent at a treatment center. They don't want to talk about it.

The young adults we interviewed talked freely about communication problems they faced as teenagers:

I would have liked to have been able to talk easier with my dad—in a more chummy way, not just 'this should be done' or 'that should be done.' "

The hardest thing to talk to parents about was relationships with boys, questions about sex. Talks on these subjects were not deep enough. I wish I could have discussed this more with my parents."

Fortunately, some families have succeeded in establishing meaningful communication, and thus common understandings, on difficult subjects. For example, about one-third of the adolescents in our study say they "have had good talks with their parents about sex." But this figure is well below the number of youth who wish they could discuss this and other troubling issues with their parents (for example, "deciding what to do with my life," "wondering how to handle my feelings"). Boys want these conversations as much as girls do. And even more than youth do, parents wish they could have such talks. In fact, 60 percent say they "definitely would like to talk more" with their children about worries and concerns, hopes and dreams. An additional 37 percent said they "probably" would welcome such opportunities.

Decline in Interest

Since it is evident that family closeness requires communication between members, it is important to note that youth's interest in discussing adolescent issues with their parents steadily declines between fifth grade (58 percent) and ninth grade (37 percent). The number who want more communication with their parents on five youth topics shows a marked decline (see Figure 9).

This decline may simply be a function of the growing up process: a teenager needs to mature, to become more independent, to develop a broader social network of confidants. But this process does not require breaking off communication with his or her parents. Figure 9 shows an increase in the percentage of youth who would prefer turning to both friends and parents for advice on "very important decisions" as they grow older.

Young adolescents in the Adolescent-Parent study are more parent-oriented than peer-oriented. They prefer being able to talk with their parents about issues that bother them. Grade five is a time of special opportunity for parents to help the young adolescent initiate conversations and learn how to communicate on a feeling level (see Figure 10).

As parents, we have learned that entering into meaningful conversations with adolescent children adds a new dimension to family life. At Search Institute we had a striking illustration of the excitement parents feel once conversations do begin in the home. We had just launched a project involving over 400 young people in Minneapolis and St. Paul. Its purpose was to train them in the friendship skills needed for reaching out to lonely and alienated peers. Also involved in the training were exercises in which the youth practiced starting conversations

Figure 9. Change in Youth's Desire for Communication with Parents*

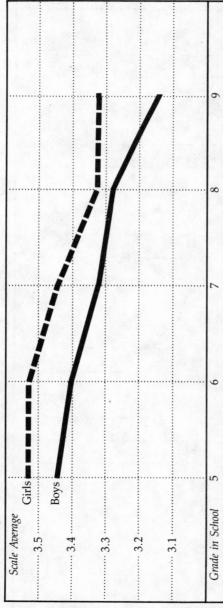

*Question: "For each of the following five items, tell if it is something you want to talk about with your parents more, less or the same as you do now." (Participants in the survey were then to answer this question for issues relating to drugs, friends, school, ideas of right and wrong, and sex.)

5 = much more
4 = a little more
3 = about the same
2 = a little less
1 = much less

Figure 10. Sources of Advice: Peers vs. parents*

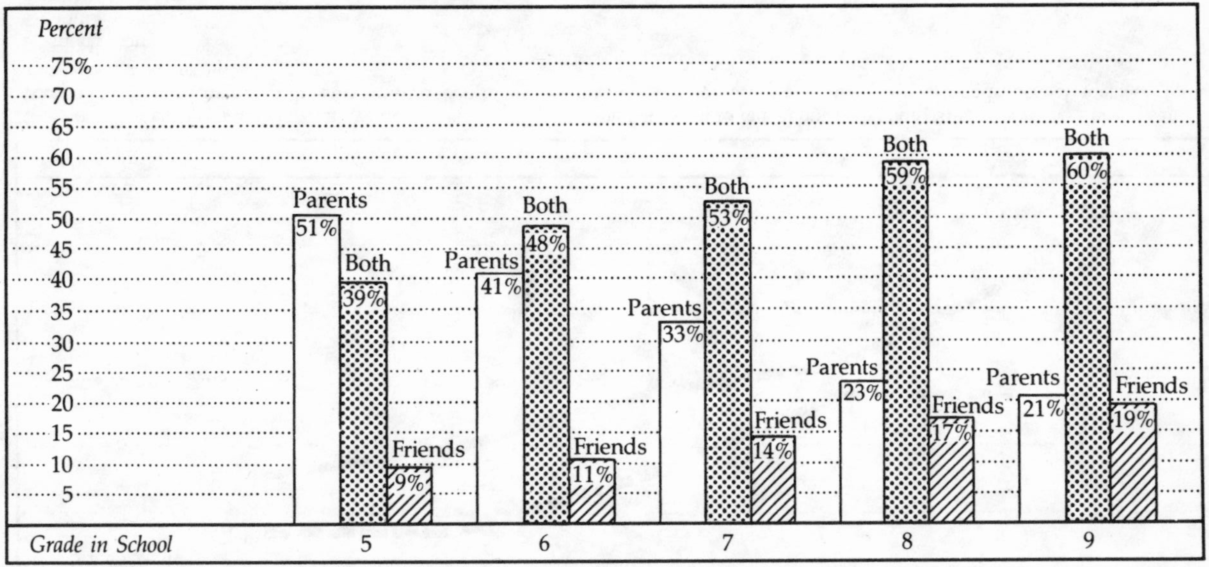

Item: "If you had a very important decision to make, to whom would you turn for advice—your friends or parents?" *Parents*—I'd turn to my parents; *Both*—I'd turn to both my parents and my friends; *Friends*—I'd turn to my friends.

with strangers and "authority figures" (parents and teachers). We wanted parents to feel comfortable with what was being done and therefore invited them to an open house. They could meet the training faculty and raise whatever questions they might have about the project.

We didn't know how many parents would come to our sessions, offered on two consecutive evenings, and planned to serve coffee and cookies for fifty people. To our surprise, 200 showed up, eager to learn about the project. Why? One after another said, "Whatever are you doing in this project? My child has actually initiated conversations in our home! We've had some long talks as a result. We love it! Keep it up!"

This incident convinced us that aided by some training, conversations can take place in the home with initiative being taken either by parent or adolescent.

Four Aids to Parent-Youth Communication

Four aids to parent-youth communication deserve mention here:

- Recognize the natural blocks to communication
- Take time to establish relationships
- Share thoughts and feelings
- Focus on the adolescent's concerns and interests

Recognize the Natural Communication Blocks. It is difficult to initiate communication with an adolescent because of certain traits that characterize adolescence itself.

1. *Growing self-consciousness.* As noted in the previous chapter, adolescents are preoccupied with themselves, and for good reason. They are trying to understand the enormous physical changes occurring within them—changes that often make them feel self-conscious. Anything that could be interpreted as a criticism or correction makes them feel as though they have been slapped on a sunburned back. This touchiness is too easily interpreted by a parent as a signal to "leave me alone."

In reality, the adolescent's hypersensitivity only underscores the need for the listening stance described in Chapter 3.

2. *Limited verbal skills.* A second roadblock to parent-youth communication is the difficulty adolescents, particularly boys, experience in describing feelings and emotions.

As parents we can help our adolescents develop this ability. Simply asking a "feeling" question, such as, "How do you feel about . . . ?" may open new dimensions in conversation. One father tried this technique one day when his ninth-grade son came home from school. The father asked him about his *feelings* concerning a disturbing situation that had come up in class. To his amazement, his son answered him on that level—about his feelings. "We talked for two hours!" said the father. "This has never happened before." Engaging one's adolescent in conversation requires patience, time, and the choice of a nonthreatening situation for conversation. These facts all help establish more comfortable communication and a closer parent-child relationship.

3. *Growing resistance to authority.* Parents also need to realize that an adolescent's desire to make personal decisions increases with age. Though the Adolescent-Parent study indicated only small increases in the percentage who disagree with parental rules, there is an increase from fifth to ninth grade in the percentage who reject authority. Thus it would seem that when an adolescent exhibits growing resistance to authority within the family structure, parents should make sure they talk with the child on a peer level. This kind of relationship reduces the social distance—and the defenses—between parent and adolescent. Children whose parents relate to them as peers, regardless of age, often refer to their mother or father as "a friend" or "my best friend." The beauty of this relationship is that it can begin early and endure for life. Very young children blossom when they are spoken to without condescension, as people whose opinions and ideas are respected and listened to.

Take Time to Establish Relationships. Over half (53 percent) of the adolescents in the Adolescent-Parent study spend less than 30 minutes a day with their fathers; and 44 percent spend less than 30 minutes with their mothers. That's the same amount of time parents take for watching the news on TV. Even more alarming, one-fourth of the ninth-graders in this study spend less than five minutes (on an average day) alone with father to talk, play, or just be together. No doubt this neglect is one reason why 46 percent of the fathers in the study admit they worry ("quite a bit" or "very much") about how their child feels about them.

The following story of Paul Tsongas, as told by Ellen Goodman in the *Boston Globe*, is a poignant and heartwarming illustration of how a man regards time with his family as a top priority.

I met Paul Tsongas once on a late-afternoon flight from Washington to Boston. The senator from Massachusetts was traveling light that day. No bags, no briefcase, no aides. All he had with him was a daughter.

It was rare enough to see a man alone on a plane with a preschool child. But Tsongas's reason was even more unusual. He was going to Boston for a meeting and he wanted to spend some time with his middle daughter. So he was taking her along for the ride. Together they would get the late plane back.

I've thought about that scene a dozen times, with mixed feelings of admiration and poignancy. Here was a father struggling with the demands of work and family. Here was a father who had to capture minutes with his child, on the fly, at 35,000 feet.

This scene, repeated over and again in Tsongas's life, seems somehow symbolic of a whole generation of men and women: parents with schedule books. It is barely even a parody of the way many of us cram work and children into calendars that won't expand to fill the needs, into lives that cry out for more hours. Tsongas was one of us, trying to make it all fit together.

But last October, the senator and father of three young girls discovered something that wasn't on his agenda. He had a tumor that was "not benign." . . . The statistical average life expectancy for those with this disease (mild lymphoma), as he related it, is eight years, and he is planning for more. . . . But Tsongas decided not to run again. He is coming home to Lowell, Mass., and home to his family in a way that politics doesn't allow.

. . . Tsongas never forgot the older colleague who stopped by his table when he was a freshman congressman and said, "Let me tell you one thing. I was in your shoes. I was here and I really devoted myself to my job and I ignored my kids and they grew up and I never knew them. It makes me very sad. Whatever you do, don't do that."

[Tsongas] had to hear the words "not benign" to finally focus on priorities, on mortality, on time itself. . . . There are times when we all end up completing a day or a week or a month, as if it were a task to be crossed off the list with a sign. In the effort to make it all work, it can become all work. We become one-minute managers, mothers, husbands. We end up spending our time on the fly.[6]

As Paul Tsongas did that day on the plane, a number of parents arrange for special time when *one* child is "alone" with *one* parent. This time alone together is important for building self-confidence in the adolescent. It is, however, of the essence in this kind of setup that the parent shows no partiality, and attempts to make each child's time equal in amount or quality.

In Charlie Shedd's book *Promises to Peter*, he relates that during his children's growing-up years he took each child out for dinner—alone—monthly. The kids chose the restaurant. After they'd had a good talk, they went to the dime store and picked out something they wanted. Shedd says that even when his children reached adolescence, when they didn't talk much to the family, they still enjoyed these monthly talks with their father.[7]

Some parents arrange for regular times when the family discusses any issues they wish. In this way, parents come to understand what their children are thinking on personal matters, the church, the community, and the world.

In thinking about taking time to be with our children, it is well to remind ourselves also that *listening*, of which we spoke at some length in Chapter 3, is a vital form of communication, even though it is basically silent.

Share Thoughts and Feelings. Some parents find it hard to admit to their adolescent that they have personal struggles and failures, too. The young woman in the following illustration wishes her father could have shared some of his inner struggles with her and her sister during their teen years. Because he did not, the father and the younger sister went through some rough years of alienation. Said the young woman,

When I was an adolescent, my father seemed to us to be strong, domineering, opinionated, sarcastic, ambitious, and successful. Since I have become an adult, my father has shared some of his fears and problems with us. I wish he could have been like that when my sister and I were teenagers at home.

The very nature of the early relationship between parent and child dictates that the parent controls most situations and decisions. Thus the parent may feel that he or she cannot reveal weaknesses or talk about personal problems; this, the parent reasons, might weaken the traditional position of authority, confuse the child, or make the child think the parent is inadequate. But it seems important that this stance change so that both parent and the child are free to reveal their humanness, their capacity for failure and struggle. That is a vital part of parent-youth communication, one that creates an attitude of mutual understanding and trust.

Some parents find it difficult to verbalize their love for their children. Strangely, the existence of love cannot be assumed. If it is unspoken, it may be doubted. Parents need to tell their children they love them. A counselor speaks of being in his office one day with a small family group troubled with parent-child conflicts. Suddenly the father turned angrily to his teenage son and said, "But you *know* I love you." To which the young man replied with equal emotion, "No, I don't. You've given me just about everything I've ever wanted, but I don't remember you *ever* telling me that you loved me!"

Some parents find it difficult to receive correction or insight from their teenager. Actually, teenagers may be very helpful to a parent in giving both negative and positive insights.

I well remember the time when one of our teenage sons said to me, "Mom, there's something I want to tell you. I hardly ever hear you saying bad things about people, but your tone of voice changes when you talk about certain kinds of people. I can tell that you think of them in a belittling way and it bothers me."

This was a jolting critique. In this situation, it would have been easy for me to have become defensive and counter with, "You're a fine one to talk. You've got some shaping up to do yourself." Instead, I asked him to clarify and give an example of what he meant. He did. It was a humbling and helpful insight.

Focus on Their Concerns and Interests. Adolescents want to talk about the very issues parents wish could be discussed, namely, their worries (See Table 3). For parents, these concerns can provide openings to discuss numerous topics. One thoughtful young man whose father was a reserved, busy

Table 3. The Worries of Young Adolescents

Percent responding *very much* or *quite a bit*

Item	All Youth	Grade 5	Grade 6	Grade 7	Grade 8	Grade 9
School performance	57%	54%	54%	57%	59%	60%
About my looks	53	42	48	56	60	57
How well other kids like me	48	43	46	51	50	48
Parent might die	47	50	48	49	47	41
How my friends treat me	45	42	43	46	47	45
Hunger and poverty in U.S.	38	52	41	39	32	31
Violence in U.S.	36	43	37	38	33	30
Might lose best friend	36	40	35	39	34	29
Drugs and drinking	35	40	38	35	33	32
Might not get good job	30	31	28	31	28	30
Physical development	26	31	28	27	24	17
Nuclear destruction of U.S.	25	29	28	27	22	21
Parents might divorce	22	30	26	22	17	13
That I may die soon	21	26	24	24	17	13
Sexual abuse	19	24	21	19	17	15
Friends will get me in trouble	18	25	21	18	13	13
Drinking by a parent	15	21	18	14	11	11
Get beat up at school	12	18	16	12	9	9
Physical abuse by parent	12	17	13	12	9	9
That I might kill myself	12	16	12	11	9	9

school administrator, regretted that during his adolescent years he saw his father as aloof, not really interested in him. He knows now that this observation was wrong. But consequently, this young man has a strong feeling that a parent must be aware that a young person often has neither the courage nor the know-how to *initiate* conversation about his or her worries. To adolescents, personal problems are mountainous obstacles; they are afraid parents will consider these same problems as insignificant, and so the parents are never made aware of the worries and given a chance to help.

One woman remembers as a teenager trying to get up enough courage to approach her mother on a question about sex. "If only there had been a word, a 'lead' on my mother's part," she said, "the floodgates of sharing a painful problem would have been released." A general question or comment on any one of the following topics may become the occasion for a good conversation.

1. *School performance.* Fifth-graders especially want to talk about the top worry of young adolescents: "How I'm doing in school." It is important for them to make their parents proud by doing well both at school and in extracurricular activities. They even want to talk with their parents about trouble at school. If parents do not make use of this chance for open, two-way conversations, it will be more difficult in the years ahead—especially with boys, whose desire to do well in school declines as they near the ninth grade.

2. *My looks.* Worry about one's physical appearance, the second greatest worry of young adolescents, reaches its highest point among eighth-grade girls. Among fifth-graders, "looks" rates seventh as a worry. Because teenagers are preoccupied with how they look to their peers, fads in clothes and styles need not be a subject of parental censure. Rather, the parent might make efforts to affirm those styles that compliment the adolescent. The question parents might ask themselves here is, "So what if I don't like that outfit? Is it worth breaking a relationship to get my way?" Chances are good that the fad

will assume its proper perspective for the adolescent if the parent doesn't nag about it.

Since looks are a concern, parents might do well to open doors for positive interchange if an adolescent in the family is, for instance, overweight. No amount of nagging or ridicule will help. But talking frankly about the struggles of dieting, affirming positive features—these are the gifts of communication a parent can bring to these situations.

3. *That a parent might die.* This fear, high among fifth- and sixth-graders and ninth-grade girls, touches a tender part of the spirit. Adolescents are often afraid to tell their parents about this fear. Such was the case with one of our sons, who remembers as a fifth-grader "standing by the window for what seemed like hours waiting for you to get home. If it got late, I was sure you had been killed in a car accident." Verbal expression of fears such as this present an opening for caring communication between parent and child.

4. *How friends treat me.* This fifth-ranked worry mounts each year to its highest peak among 45 percent of eighth-graders. Parents might use this concern as the basis for discussing with the adolescent what it means to be a friend to someone else, shifting the emphasis away from "what my friend can give to me" to "what I can give my friend."

The problem of being "picked on" and getting into a fight is a great worry to fifth- and sixth-graders. Instead of getting angry at the child or at the others who involved the adolescent in a fight, a parent may find in this situation an opportunity to learn how the fight started and what are the child's feelings about the incident.

6. *Hunger and poverty.* Interestingly, this is the number-one worry of fifth-graders in the Adolescent-Parent study, suggesting how conscious they are of the suffering of others. Significantly, the worry declines with age, and becomes sixth-ranked for those in grades seven to nine. This subject, which parallels a comparable decline in concern for people, will be considered again in Chapter 6.

7. *Violence in our country.* Again, fifth graders—the "worry-warts" among adolescents—are most conscious of this problem. In ways parents might not expect, adolescents of this age are very aware of their community and nation. Current events could well be topics at the dinner table. Fears about incidents of violence might be brought into the open. If local incidents of violence have occurred, parents might discuss safety measures in the home and rules for self-protection.

8. *Lose best friend.* This eighth-ranked worry peaks for seventh-graders and declines to its lowest point among ninth-graders. The concern is closely related to "how other kids like me" and "how my friends treat me." It is a reflection of the adolescent's longing to be seen as a "fun" person, a significant person. A teacher says, "One of the most painful things I see in a classroom is the cruel ways teenagers treat each other, and especially the one who is on the fringe of things." Parents do well not to ignore a child's "loss of a best friend." By conveying the impression that "This is kid stuff," a parent shuts the door to good conversations on subjects of self-image and sharing feelings with others.

9. *Drinking by friends.* This is a genuine worry for 35 percent of the youth in our study, one which adolescents would prefer to discuss with their parents. Surprisingly, those most worried about the subject are sixth-graders. Most parents do not see their sixth-graders as being old enough to talk about the use of alcohol; but the results of the Adolescent-Parent study, as well as many others, indicate that this age is crucial for discussion on this topic. The adolescent's concern here may be a mingling of worry about peer relationships, peer pressures, and the tremendous battle of ambivalence: "My parents don't like this," or "What if the kids get me to do it?" or "Does it mean I can't go out with my friends to parties?" or "Should I try it?" Girls especially want parental communication on this subject.

10. *Locating a job.* Even among early adolescents, vocational goals are important, and with this concern comes worry about

not being able to "get a good job when I am older." This tenth-ranked worry is highest for ninth-graders. It is wise for a parent to find out how much importance the adolescent attaches to advanced education and then, depending on the ability and interest of the young person, discuss the value of working for a junior college degree, a vocational technical degree, or a higher degree.

One young adult tells of his parents taking him as a teen-ager to the Mayo Clinic for a visit, because he had expressed a strong desire to study medicine. Some parents arrange to have their son or daughter meet a person who is in a vocation that interests the child. Parents and adolescents grow in understanding of each other as they explore the question, "How does one develop one's career potential?" Everyone knows that adolescents' ideas on vocation may, and most likely will, change many times before adulthood. This process, however, is an important beginning in learning to make decisions.

Parental Discipline or Control

A third major factor in close family life is parental discipline. How parents treat their children powerfully shapes not only the emotional climate of the home, but also the children's personality, character, and competence. In the Adolescent-Parent study a shift occurs in type of discipline as the adolescents grew older. Ninth-graders report more inflexible or autocratic treatment from their parents, another factor that contributes to a decline in family closeness. Parental control is an important factor in how parents and adolescents relate to each other.

Through careful studies, Diana Baumrind was able to identify three types of parental discipline and demonstrate how each disciplinary pattern shapes the child in a different way. Data from the study of 10,467 parents confirm that these three types of discipline are being used in families: autocratic, permissive, and democratic (authoritative); each is associated with contrasting kinds of behavior. The first two methods create

distance between parents and adolescents, whereas the third—
the democratic or authoritative—encourages family closeness.
Parents who value a close family life might well evaluate the
approach they now use. The way parents treat their children
either inclines them toward a loving response or toward a
rebellious rejection of behavior that the parents may idealize.

Autocratic-Type Discipline

Baumrind identifies the authoritarian (hereafter referred to
as an autocratic) parent as one who values obedience as a
virtue and favors punitive or forceful methods to curb the self-
will of a child.[8] The parent does not encourage verbal give-
and-take, believing rather that the child should always accept
the parent's position as right. Autocratic parents may be either
very protective or very neglectful.

Although many of the 10,467 parents in this study are inclined toward the autocratic stance, it is a matter of degree;
some parents are more rigid, controlling, and demanding than
others. When it comes to verbal give-and-take, one in ten say
it "often" happens that "I will not allow my child to question
the rules I make." Three in ten say it happens "sometimes."

Similarly, 14 percent of the mothers and 20 percent of the
fathers say it happens "often" that "I do not let my child
question my decisions." An additional three in ten say this
happens "sometimes."

The clearest expression of an autocratic parent comes in the
response given to the survey item, "I expect my child to
believe I am always right."

One in five mothers (19 percent) and one in four fathers (25
percent) say they "often" take this position. If we include the
"sometimes" response, we find half of the parents trying to
give children the impression of being "always right." This
need may stem from the idea that admission of error by parents weakens their authority.

Parents who "overcontrol" usually punish for wrong behavior. Here is how parents in the study thought they would react

when presented with the following imaginary situation: If their adolescent (age ten to fourteen) came home at 10:30 P.M., though the curfew was clearly understood to be 9:00 P.M., 34 percent said they "probably" would yell at their child; 7 percent were "very sure" they would yell. Yelling suggests anger, and is a common response of autocratic parents. One third of the parents (33 percent) admit to times when they get so angry they are afraid they might hurt their child. This strong response reminds us of how much an autocratic approach is linked with personal feelings or reactions to stress. Findings in *Study of Generations* show that parents who are autocratic in treatment of their children tend also to be law-oriented in their understanding of religion.[9] This means they view Christianity as basically a set of rules and standards that must be obeyed. Such parents find it hard to forgive and hard to admit they are wrong. Their religion tends to be self-centered and self-serving.

The issue of the autocratic parent appeared prominently in our study of 7,050 high school youth (discussed in *Five Cries of Youth*). Two out of five young people (39 percent) were bothered either "very much" or "quite a bit" by the fact that "My parents are too strict." In that study we found that one result of extreme strictness was greater tension in the home. In comparisons between groups, we found greater family disunity and more distance between parents and youth in the families of overly strict parents than any other group. We found the effect of overcontrol on youth to be lower self-esteem and heightened feelings of self-condemnation. Another frequent outcome is parent-youth conflict, with life in the home becoming an ongoing power struggle.[10]

Similar effects are seen in our analyses of data from the Adolescent-Parent study. Adolescents raised under autocratic control are more likely to be characterized by the following behaviors: hostility to parents; age prejudice; antisocial activities (for example, stealing, lying, fighting, vandalism); feelings of social alienation; rejection of traditional moral standards;

and inability to relate well to people. An overly strict approach also encourages a more prejudicial and judgmental spirit in the adolescent.

These outcomes are similar to those reported in many other studies. Punitive approaches to discipline—including verbal and physical abuse, and unreasonable deprivations of privilege—have negative effects. More of the children in homes characterized by this approach react with attitudes of noncompliance and a compulsion to transgress.

Permissive-Type Discipline

It must not be inferred from the above comments that parents should operate without controls. Permissiveness in discipline can be as negative in its effect on children (and on close family life) as an autocratic approach.

Baumrind identified a permissive parent as one who sees him or herself as a resource to be used as the child wishes—not as one responsible for shaping the child's future behavior. The immediate aim of such a parent is to free the child from restraint and allow the child to develop as he or she chooses.[11] Whereas the autocratic parent expects a child to act as an adult, the permissive parent believes the child should have all the privileges of an adult.

A fair number of the 10,467 parents in the study lean toward permissive parenting. When asked, "How often is it true that you 'let your child do whatever he or she wants to do'?" a little over one-third (37 percent) said "often" or "very often." A total of 22 percent acknowledge being "too lenient"; and about that many (20 percent) admitted "I often let my child off easy."

This approach of under-control has its negative effects. Children who live in overly permissive homes have trouble believing their parents really care about them. Permissiveness is sometimes interpreted as a form of rejection. This may be one of the reasons that our measures show that a number of negative behavior patterns are associated with a permissive approach. Adolescents whose parents assume little responsibility for their behavior show more of the following characteristics: Fewer are likely to go out of their way to help people (helping a peer with homework, mowing lawns for those who cannot do it themselves, helping someone pick up dropped groceries); fewer are willing to live by the moral standards of their parents (with respect to stealing, lying, drinking); more are likely to become involved in hedonistic behavior (use and abuse of alcohol, sex, drugs); more will seek out movies that are sexually explicit and erotic. Permissiveness seems to encourage a hedonistic and antisocial behavior that brings its own tragedies. Clearly, a child needs firm limits.

More important than these negative behaviors is the loss of desired, positive behaviors. Adolescents of parents who use permissive-type discipline are not as likely to be concerned about people, to relate well to others, or to be religiously or ethically motivated.

Authoritative (Democratic) Discipline

The disciplinary approach that seems to work the best falls between autocratic and permissive. We use the terms "authoritative" and "democratic" to describe this third form of parenting. The firmness of an authoritative parent is combined with the freedom found in a democratic setting. The parent who uses the authoritative approach exerts firm control; at the same time, this parent does not hem the child in with restrictions; he or she values both independence in the child and disciplined conformity. The authoritative parent affirms a child's own qualities and style; at the same time, this parent sets standards for future conduct.

The comments of a young adult, reminiscing about his upbringing, reflect this balance: "In our family, there was a delicate balance between allowing the children to make mistakes and be their own person on the one hand, and setting helpful, protective boundaries and values for them on the other hand."

One indication of the number of parents in our study who

use this authoritative approach to parenting is found in their response to the item, "I give my child a chance to talk over rules he or she does not like or understand." Over half say they do this "often"; of these, 18 percent said they do this "very often."

Three out of four parents say it is "often true" that "When I tell my child I am going to punish him or her, I follow through and do it." Whether or not practice is equal to report we do not know. But clearly half or more identify themselves as having characteristics of an authoritative approach to discipline.

Baumrind concludes, on the basis of her research on preschool children, that authoritative patterns of upbringing are more beneficial to children than autocratic and permissive patterns.[12] From our analyses of Adolescent-Parent data, we come to the same conclusion about young adolescents. The children of parents using the democratic or authoritative approach to discipline are more likely to be service-oriented, concerned about people, free from feelings of alienation, and committed to a religious faith. Where this approach to family discipline is used, one is more likely to find family closeness, parental affection, and parental reward-giving.

A striking illustration of the contrasting effects of the autocratic-permissive versus authoritative (democratic) approaches to parenting is seen in a study of college students. Its purpose was to see if there was any connection between parents' use of social control and their offspring's involvement with marijuana. The findings showed high use of marijuana by students whose parents were perceived to have been permissive, and medium use among students who saw their parents as autocratic. The students for whom use of marijuana was low perceived their parental relationship as democratic. The researcher saw the parent-child interaction, parents' respect for the child's participation, and the mutual sharing and listening stance of the democratic parental relationship as fostering a personal commitment to the values of the parents.[13]

Guidelines for Practical Applications of Authoritative (Democratic)-Discipline

Based on this analysis of parental discipline styles, we think that the following guidelines show the kinds of parenting that make for a close family.

1. *An adolescent needs clear, firmly established rules.* This means a clear definition of acceptable and unacceptable conduct, as well as a clear statement of consequences if the rule is broken. Interestingly, young adolescents in the study do not rebel against parental rules. Acceptance of rules remains the same from the fifth to the ninth grades, even though there is an increase in resistance to authority over these years.

2. *A flexible stance, blended with good judgment, is important.* A young adult recalls an experience in his teen years:

My friend and I took our family boat without asking permission of our parents, and I was grounded for a month. I became rebellious because I felt it was too strong a punishment. My parents, when they saw my reaction, lowered the punishment. I think this was very important. Parents need to be flexible when the situation warrants it.

A mother says:

If you realize you have made a wrong decision about something involving your child, be willing to change that decision, if need be. What I do first, if the child thinks it is unfair, is tell him I will think about changing it. Then I come to him later and tell him I have done so.

3. *Consistency in defining and applying discipline is essential.* In a supermarket one day, we heard a classic illustration of inconsistency in discipline. The characters in this minidrama were a mother with two young children:

"Brian, if you don't behave, I'm going to put you and Susie out in the car."

Less than a minute later:

"If you don't do what I say, I'm never going to take you shopping again."

One aisle later:

"Brian, if you don't come right over here, I'm going to spank you."

A confused concept of what the parent wants and expects, and a confused concept of punishment is disturbing to a child. Preliminary findings from Francis J. Ianni's recent eight-year study on adolescents show that most teenagers studied were looking for consistent rules in families, schools and communities. "In fact," says Ianni, "they are often desperately seeking those rules."

His study attempted to determine what rules parents, school officials, and others in a community thought they were imposing on the adolescents. The initial studies were in a New York City neighborhood where residents were poor and mostly black, Hispanic, or Chinese. In urban settings the researchers found families, schools, social agencies, and criminal justice workers in conflict, often blaming each other for society's failures. As a result, these institutions set highly conflicting rules for teenagers, who responded to them with resistance and rejection. It is out of this conflict that street gangs emerge "almost destined," says Ianni, "to put these kids in future conflict with society." He adds, "But there is a consistent set of rules to follow."[14]

4. *Disciplining must be a private affair.* To be humiliated or embarrassed in front of friends or in a public place touches one of the most sensitive spots for an adolescent, namely, concern about the opinion of others, especially peers. The humiliation from such an experience can linger on into marriage situations and become one of the "wounded memories" referred to in Chapter 2. This is evident in a husband's words to his wife one evening after she had taken issue with him in front of a social group, "When you criticize me in front of others, it touches something very painful for me, since I was shamed frequently as a kid, and I feel like hiding."[15]

5. *The use of sarcasm or "rubbing it in" brings negative results.* One teenager said,

When I do admit I was wrong about something or say I'm sorry, my parents cut me down. They say, "Oh, she admitted she was wrong? Mark that on a calendar . . . " or something like that. And it makes me feel bad and makes me not want to talk to them.[16]

To "rub it in" and not allow the adolescent to forget that he or she transgressed drives children and parents apart. Sometimes these cutting words, often spoken in front of others, pretend to be in jest, but their meaning is clear. The adolescent has every right to ask that it be stopped.

6. *Conflict can be handled in a positive way.* It is easy for parents to withdraw or react angrily when a teenager espouses a value different from that of the parent. Even though hurt, afraid, angry, and disappointed, parents cannot afford to panic in such a situation and thus allow communication to break off. When adolescents know that their parents are trying to understand and appreciate their feelings, even if they don't sanction the behavior, a spirit of closeness develops between generations.

Even in "ordinary" arguments, in which a break between generations is not imminent, it is important to state clearly to each other what has been the cause of irritation, and to try to work for a solution. A young woman, looking back on her teen years, speaks rather wistfully:

When there was an argument at home (and there were many), nobody would speak to each other for about two days. It was awful. Then we'd get friendly again, but there was no settling of anything, no resolving of issues.

Parental Nurturance

Nurturance has been defined as caretaking—parental acts and attitudes of love that are directed at enhancing the well-being of the child. We found in the Adolescent-Parent study that nurturance is a powerful force for good. Adolescents in homes characterized by love and affectionate caring are better able to resist negative behaviors and more free to develop in positive ways. For instance, there is significantly less social alienation among adolescents whose parents emphasize nurturance, as well as less involvement in drug or alcohol use and sexual activity. In nurturing homes we find more adolescents who know how to make friends and maintain good relationships with them; more who are involved in helping-type behaviors and more who tend to view religion as a liberating and challenging force in their lives.

Although nurturance can be expressed in many ways, we have chosen to discuss it under the following headings:

- Showing affection
- Building trust
- Doing things together
- Developing support systems.

Showing Affection

The decline in family closeness discussed at the beginning of this chapter is paralleled by a decline in how often parents show affection to adolescents. When asked, "How often do you say things to your child like 'I love you' or 'I'm proud of you'?" parents' answers show a dramatic decline by year in school, as seen in Table 4.

As one would surmise, the percent who express this verbal affection only four times a month (or less) increases with each year in school.

Table 5 illustrates that decline also occurs with measures of touching, caressing, and embracing. For some reason, parents

Table 4. Parents Expressing Verbal Affection Every Day

Child's Grade in School	Mothers	Fathers
5	61%	40%
6	57	37
7	50	30
8	45	29
9	37	24

become less affectionate as their children enter the adolescent period.

Table 5. Parents Expressing Physical Affection Every Day

Child's Grade in School	Mothers	Fathers
5	83%	64%
6	75	59
7	67	47
8	60	43
9	49	33

Nonverbal communication is important in expressing closeness. Holding a child's hand, stroking hair or forehead, leaning over to put a hand on the shoulder are examples of gestures that create strong bonds and often speak louder than words. A touch can say "I care," "I love you," "I'm here." Every parent needs to find a way of showing affection that is natural and comfortable for both parent and child.

Demonstrating affection is not always easy for parents. Perhaps it was not done in their own parental homes. Yet many parents wish they could free themselves to express affection toward their adolescent. Said one father, "I would be a better parent if I could express myself more freely with hugs and kisses."

This parent is right. He would be filling a definite need in his adolescent's emotional development if he could show affection. Figure 11 shows evidence that fathers are less demonstrative in showing affection than are mothers. Expressions of love and caring are especially needed from both parents during the adolescent period. Struggling to know who they are and how they are regarded by others, adolescents need the affirmation found in both verbal and nonverbal physical signs that they are loved.

Building Trust

Respect for the privacy of adolescents, an important aspect of nurturance, indicates parents' belief in their children's right

Figure 11. Change in Demonstrative Affection by Parents*

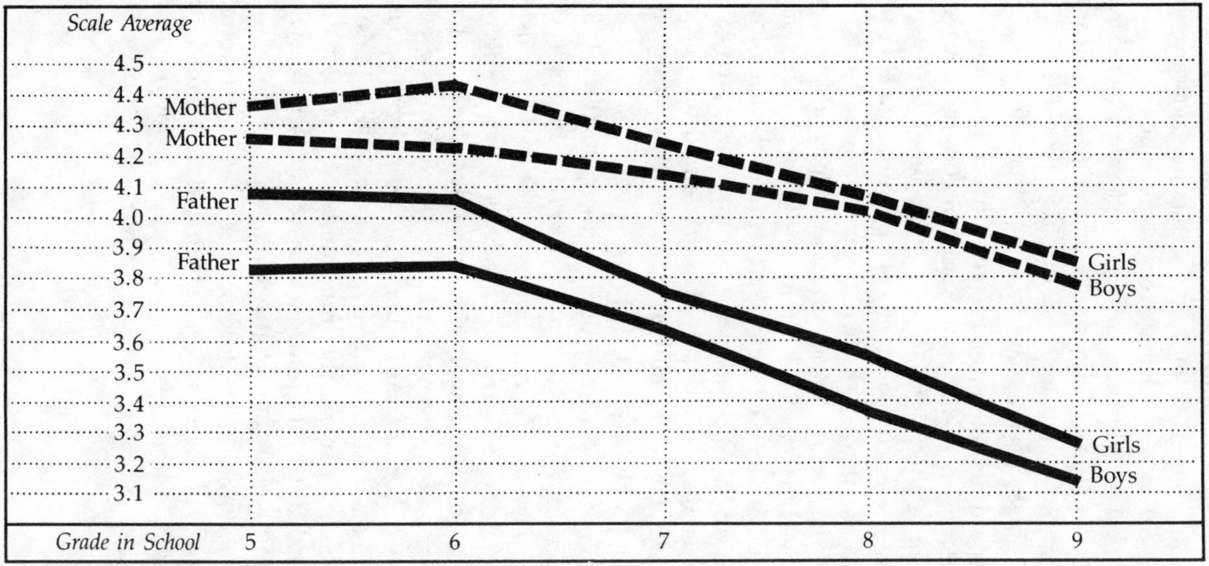

*Item: "How often does your mother/father hug or kiss you?"

5 = Daily
4 = Couple of times a week
3 = One to four times a month
2 = Less than once a month
1 = Never

to have a life space of their own. More than that, it is an important ingredient in building trust. Parents who listen to phone conversations or open and read letters are violating the adolescent's desire not to reveal every aspect of himself or herself to others. Throwing out clothes, magazines, or records belonging to the adolescent, or going through desk and dresser drawers, are actions that often result in alienation instead of togetherness. What is needed are trust-building efforts.

Adolescents' strong desire for privacy surfaced in a survey done by Jane Norman and Myron Harris in conjunction with Xerox Education Publications in 1977. Out of 673,479 early adolescents (ages eight to fourteen), 41 percent said that if a parent violated the privacy of their room they would discuss the issue with the parent; 26 percent said they would use the "hide and lock technique." The remaining participants said they would retaliate in kind or make a scene when the invasions occurred. In this questionnaire, Norman and Harris also learned that teenagers get upset when parents do not affirm and enforce each family members' right to privacy from siblings as well as parents.[17]

"Snooping parents" basically distrust their children. When trust is not present, relationship deteriorates. In *Traits of a Healthy Family*, Dolores Curran reports that a *sense of trust* is rated number four by 551 survey respondents.[18] Jerry M. Lewis, author of *No Single Thread*, a significant work on healthy families, found that parents from such families have a strong need to *preserve trust*, and that family trust itself begins with spousal trust. Building trust in a family begins early in the life of a child. Yet for many parents the importance of this trait does not become real until the first instances of broken trust between them and their teenager appear.[19]

If respect for private life and time space is worked through, the family has a better chance of staying close through the adolescent years. As one teenager remarked about the home she would like to have some day, "I'd like it to be close *and* open."

Doing Things Together. Love and caring is shown by taking an interest in the activities of one's children and doing things together with them. Interestingly, there is no appreciable decline in the number of hours families spend each week in doing things together. Apparently, patterns established when the children are young are maintained as they enter the adolescent period. It is significant, however, that about one-third (36 percent) of the families in the Adolescent-Parent study spend less than five hours in an average week doing things together.

Perhaps in our culture, family time together is possible only if a conscious decision is made to find time. Just as a budget is planned, so time together needs to be planned. Hamilton McCubbin and David Olson,[20] in their study of families that cope well under stress, found that one characteristic of such families is "they set aside time to be together." A tremendous learning opportunity is created by the family which discusses and prioritizes its family time.

One of our sons recalls how this was done in our family:

We set aside a definite evening for planning, with all family members participating, giving their suggestions as to what they would like to do. Granted, some plans did not work out, but we had a fail-safe. Sunday noon dinners, which were our council time, were occasions for regrouping.

Even though mealtimes have traditionally been "together" times, there are evidences that American families are robbing themselves of this valuable time for talking and listening to each other. Fast-food dining is becoming an American way of life, a symbol of shortness and intensity in our social encounters. Work schedules and organized activities are culprits in limiting family mealtimes, and perhaps television viewing is equally guilty.

Author George Armelagos[21] reminisces about the significance of the dinner hour in the past. He regards it as having been one of the major times that the parents included children in family and societal affairs. Often dinner began with a prayer, which then put the food in a symbolic and ritualistic context. In the process of talking during the meal, social relationships, attitudes and beliefs were all enforced.

Armelagos expresses sadness over the death of the family table. Yet parents who care about the values of doing things together have it in their power to reverse this decline in their own home.

When interviewed, a number of young adults and adolescents alike speak of certain mealtimes during the week as being a highlight in family memories. This is especially interesting because therapists often ask a patient to think back to his or her memory of a family dinner during childhood. It is a way of finding out how much general communication and interaction there was in a patient's early life. Therapists maintain that there is a relationship between the love in a home and the richness of the family table experience. "It is to the table that love or discord eventually come."

As parents, our image of teenagers is frequently that they are champing the bit to throw off some of the traditions of home, those hundreds of little rituals of togetherness unique to each family. Sometimes when children leave home and establish their own families, they perpetuate traditions that did not seem to interest them when they were living at home. In our own family, with its Scandinavian roots, we have a tradition of serving lutefisk each Christmas Eve. To our knowledge, our second-oldest son never deigned to taste it. But a year after he was married, we had a long-distance call from South Dakota: "Say, how do you prepare lutefisk?"

Teens may go through a period of pulling away. They are, after all, in a separation process. But ultimately, when they form a new family, some old and some new traditions will be part of their lives. Every experience parents give their children becomes part of their future. It will be heartwarming for parents to note that, when interviewed, adolescents and young adults alike listed as most important, regardless of the activity, ingredients such as these: "we were all together," "Dad played with us," "we joked and laughed a lot," "we talked about funny things that happened in our family," "we all went and helped somebody," "our parents let us work with them on fixing things."

A recurring theme of these interviews was the memory of Christmas:

We lived on a farm, and I remember my sister and I going with my mother every Christmas Eve to a neighbor's home. They were very poor. Mother always made special food for that family. I try to do things like that myself every Christmas—and other times, too.

Vacations are special times too. One of our sons shared the following insight:

Family vacations have been very important in our family. When I think of how they have helped shape me, I would say that going to new exciting places (as we did) together with the family has given me a powerful sense of belonging. I was co-existing with my family while at the same time branching out into unfamiliar territory. Somehow it could be seen as risk-taking with security.

Developing Support Systems

A caring family unit forms its own support group. As one young adult says, "We pull for each other." Another adds, "We have a commitment to each other."

One of our sons relates the following incident:

I remember when I was a little boy and my brothers were teenagers. We were setting camp at Mt. Rainier and I was so enthralled by the surroundings that I set out to explore them. When I realized I had gone so far that the family was nowhere in sight, I became frightened and cried out. I can still remember vividly the family converging on me. Some came running up the path. My older brother took the shortest route and climbed the cliff. I can remember seeing his face appearing over the rock. It was a warm, wonderful memory of family support.

In fact, families that report having quality relationships with relatives and friends dealt best with the stresses of family life. David Olson,[22] professor of family science at the University of Minnesota, was surprised to find how much the nuclear family of parents and children in his study relied on relatives for emotional support. Our interviews with young adults and adolescents bore out this finding:

My warmest memories are of my extended family. I was my grandfather's special person.

I like my mother's family. Somehow they always notice me at family gatherings. They make me feel important.

Our many Sunday dinners at my uncle and aunt's house said to me, "You're important to us."

When we were in very bad financial straits as a family, there would always be a substantial check for Christmas from two of my uncles.

My aunt and uncle shaped my concept of caring. When my brother, who was a teenager, was dying, they spent hours and hours at his bedside and supported our family in every possible way.

Curran, in *Traits of a Health Family*, finds that in black families particularly "grandma" establishes a close, lifelong relationship with her grandchildren, a relationship missing in many white, middle-class families. Often grandma is the early caregiver to these children whose parents, out of necessity or desire, have to go to work. The grandchildren develop a basic trust in grandma in their infancy years. As they grow up and move away, they come back for support and affirmation both from their own parents and from grandma.[23]

Community and friends are also part of the extended support systems. A young man writes,

My high school basketball coach was extended family. He was my model. He was the first person I could discuss my faith with.

Our next-door neighbors were always there if I got in trouble and my parents weren't home is the comment of another young person.

Conclusion

Close family life is one of the major sources of strength for adolescents. Measures of nurturance, authoritative (democratic) control, good family communication, and parental harmony show that this resource of family closeness gives adolescents an inner strength for growth and development as well as for more responsible living. A close family characterized by parental affection, trust, doing things together, and strong support systems provides an inner resistance to the toxins of life. It provides an atmosphere within which an adolescent best matures toward the seven developmental goals described in Chapter 3.

This resource is eroded, however, by parental disharmony and by styles of discipline that are either autocratic or permissive. Their negative effect on a family unit are too important to ignore.

The issue in this chapter is one of building close relationships. Those who work with troubled youth report that "quality of human relationships is the most powerful determinant of successful programs in the education and treatment of troubled children.[24] The principle applies to all types of adolescents. Nothing is as powerful as the love of parents. And as indicated in this chapter, love is more than feeling. It is action, and a process of giving. It is caring, feeling responsible, showing respect, and learning to know the feelings of another. Love, acceptance and understanding are not the rewards of good behavior (to be used as social reinforcers) but as prerequisites to behavior.[25]

It is love and caring that establish the setting within which adolescents come to adopt the value orientation discussed in Chapter 5, and to know and understand the liberating faith discussed in Chapter 6.

5. Cry for Moral Behavior

The human mind has no more power of inventing a new value than of imagining a new primary colour, or indeed, of creating a new sun and new sky for it to move on.

—C. S. LEWIS

"What have we done differently in raising this child than his older brothers and sisters?" ask the parents of a teenage boy.

"Maybe we babied him," suggests the father.

"Maybe we left him alone too much," says the mother.

"He's caused a lot of trouble to us." The father's voice is heavy.

"He started using drugs around ninth grade—maybe before that, for all I know. It's both drugs and alcohol now."

"You've gotten help for him?" the friend asks.

"Oh, yes," replies the mother, "a whole year, every week. We were all involved."

"But something's wrong yet." The father's voice is somber. "It's like he has no respect for us, no understanding of our problems, no appreciation of what we've done for him. It's like we're just here to pay any price he wants us to pay for what *he* is doing."

"He's downright cruel," says the mother.

The experience of these parents culminates in an anguished cry: What did we do wrong? Is it too late to develop healthy concepts of right and wrong? If children have learned it "right" in childhood, does it become unlearned? If they have learned it "wrong" in childhood, can that be changed? These cries are borne out of sleepless nights, bitterness, and heartache.

Where and how do our children find the inner conviction and strength to live moral lives?

"It's the lying I can't stand," says another mother. "My daughter goes to school in the morning and skips out as soon as she can. But she tells *me* she's gone to school all day." The mother turns to her friend, searching her eyes for an answer. "Doesn't it make any difference that you teach your child not to lie when she is small? I can't understand what has happened."

The parents in these vignettes express the dilemma being faced by countless parents: How do we cope with a child whose way of living is the opposite of what we tried to teach?

This anguished cry is real, and it is a difficult one to deal with. In this chapter, we approach the subject of moral behavior by means of these topics:

- Deciding what is moral
- Becoming concerned about two critical issues in moral behavior
- Realizing how we communicate values and beliefs
- Working to internalize moral beliefs

Deciding What Is Moral

Everyone has a different idea about how people should live their lives. Some people follow traditional moral beliefs, and others follow a morality based on personal preferences or the norms of their peer group.

The conflict between these views is one that concerns many parents.

When C. S. Lewis, Oxford don and Cambridge professor, saw traditional values being debunked as "sentimental" in an English school textbook, he became very conscious of this conflict. In a book that has now become a classic, he insists that an ethic based on "I want" (a view he found espoused in the textbook) could result in nature's conquest of man. In letting instincts become one's guide, he says further, a person loses the basis for making judgments, because instincts sometimes lead one in contradictory directions. Lewis believed separation from traditional moral values introduces the demise of humankind. Hence the title of his book, *The Abolition of Man*.[1]

Lewis contends that there never has been more than one judgment of values embedded in the civilizations of this world. This judgment is found in the writings of all time—pagan and religious alike. Whether one reads the writings of ancient Babylon, Rome, China, India, or any other civilization, one finds a moral stance that includes judgments such as the following:

- The "law" of mercy
- The "law" of magnanimity
    Generosity in forgiving
    Willingness to die for another
- The "law" of doing good
- The "law" of caring for one's family
    Duties to parents and others
    Duties to children
- The "law" of justice
    Sexual justice
    Honesty
    Justice in court
- The "law" of good faith

Over the centuries, a general consensus has evolved as to what is "good." It is morality that is refined and enhanced in the writings of the Old and New Testaments. These value judgments define the moral structure or universe within which we live. It is the conviction of C. S. Lewis that the "human mind has no more power of inventing a new value than of imagining a new primary colour, or indeed, of creating a new sun and a new sky for it to move on."

C. S. Lewis's view of morality as being mercy, justice, magnanimity, caring for one's family, and the like, draws attention to the fact that there is a moral structure to our universe.

Certain generally accepted standards of goodness and rightness in conduct or character make for happy living.

As we write this chapter, for example, a number of adults are on trial for sexual abuse of children. These adults are accused of sexual acts. If convicted, they will serve prison sentences. Sanctions against child abuse, rape, indecent exposure, polygamy, and child neglect are present in civil laws because such conduct violates community values. These values are built into the fabric of life; they are necessary if a civilization is to survive. Some of these might be called intrinsic values:

- Respect for the personal dignity and freedom of individuals
- Respect for the basic human ties of family
- Respect for the physical and psychological health of people
- Respect for the rights of individuals

Parallel with these intrinsic values are moral values:

- Fidelity—keeping promises
- Honesty—being truthful
- Sexual restraint—control of sexual appetite
- Social justice—protecting the powerless

Moral values are not matters of personal preference. Rather, they are judgments about life that every civilization has found necessary for survival. E. Stanley Jones, renowned missionary and author, once said, "We don't break the Ten Commandments. If we ignore them, they break us." Schools teach moral values when they make it clear that cheating, stealing, vandalism, and fighting are not allowed. These are accepted norms, rules, or sanctions common to schools.

A parent may wonder, however, if moral behavior is not more than conformity to the generally accepted standards of right conduct or character. Granted, many parents would be enormously relieved if their son or daughter did accept and live by these standards. But one wonders if moral behavior might be more than conformity to accepted standards of goodness and rightness of conduct.

Lawrence Kohlberg, a moral theorist, thinks so. He views moral development as reflecting six distinct levels or stages in which the first stage is being good to avoid punishment. His sixth and highest stage identifies morality with the recognition of the rights of others. This recognition of people's rights centers in the principles of fairness, justice, and respect for people. Kohlberg illustrates this concept of morality with a young man's answer to the question, "What does the word 'morality' mean to you?"

I think [morality] is recognizing the rights of individuals, not interfering with those rights. Act as fairly as you would have them treat you. It means the human being's right to do as he pleases, without interfering with somebody else's rights.[2]

A crass example of this concept of morality can be heard in comments by advocates of adolescent rights. One popular psychologist, who counsels people by the radio, said this during a broadcast:

Do not meddle in the sex life of a teenager. That is their private domain. If they wish to be sexually active, that is their right and privilege.

Carol Gilligan, in her book *In A Different Voice*, presents a contrasting view by defining morality as a feeling of responsibility for the welfare of others. In her interviews with women she finds this concept of morality emerging in a striking way. An illustration of this concept surfaces in the following interview with a twenty-five-year-old law student. He was asked, "Is everybody's opinion, with respect to moral problems, equally correct?"

No . . . There are situations in which I think there are right and wrong answers that sort of inhere to the nature of existence. We need to depend on each other, to be enriched by cooperating with other people and striving to live in harmony with everybody else, to find fulfillment in ourselves. To that end, there are right and wrong things that promote different courses of action that obviously promote or harm that goal.[3]

Gilligan champions a morality that is primarily concerned about people, those suffering and in need; a morality of trying to live responsibly and contribute to the health and well-being of others. This concept of morality equates responsibility with caring.

Kohlberg, aware of this critique, refers to her morality of responsibility as an ethic of responsible, universal love (*agape*). It involves an interpenetration of religion and ethical action which he does not view as competitive with his principle of fairness. Each needs the other.

In his discussion of the highest stage of moral development, Kohlberg wonders if there might be a seventh stage—a morality motivated by religion. Religion, he sees, helps people to be moral even though acting morally may not give the person any tangible rewards or pleasure. To him, ultimate moral maturity requires a mature solution to the question of the meaning of life.[4]

Why be moral? That is a question adolescents often ask parents. Why should I try to act in ways above the behavior of my classmates? Why should I be concerned about what is fair, right, or an expression of love?

We recognize there may be several answers to this question. But one that emerges powerfully in the studies of Search Institute is the motivation of a personal faith. Though motivation for a morality of responsibility can be a humanistic love for people, our studies show it to be strongly associated with a consciousness of God's presence.

In a 1971 study of 7,050 high school youth,[5] we found that a sense of moral responsibility strongly correlates with both a consciousness of God's presence and participation in the life of a congregation. The high correlations ($r = 0.53$ and 0.55) make it clear that for youth identified with the church, morality can be more than conformity to other people's expectations. Morality can be a life of responsible caring for others that is motivated by a personal faith. Morality can be living a life of service that gives a sense of joy and meaning in life. The focus of this concept of morality is on life-enhancing activities instead of on the "don'ts" of wrong behavior.

Becoming Concerned About Two Critical Issues in Moral Behavior

We have identified two different levels or moral behavior: (1) seeking to live according to the traditional values of a moral universe; and (2) seeking to rise above laws and human expectations to a life of responsible living. Both are important and each poses a critical issue.

The Issue Involving Traditional Moral Beliefs

Parents and youth in the Adolescent-Parent study evidenced a high degree of acceptance of the traditional moral beliefs presented in the survey. They were asked to read descriptions in paragraph form of typical situations that involve issues of public morality (e.g., shoplifting, racial discrimination, premarital intercourse) and then rate them "right" or "wrong," Nine out of ten parents agreed on the wrongness of each behavior, with one exception. On the abortion issue, almost half the parents (45 percent) either expressed uncertainty or declared abortion justifiable.

The responses of the adolescents on issues of public morality were much the same. Agreement as to what is "wrong" behavior characterized over four out of five in the study. Only on the issue of abortion was there confusion. (An average of 39 percent were "not sure" whether an abortion was "right" or "wrong.") However, there was a change in perception from fifth to ninth grade—the percent "not sure" decreased from 48 percent to 34 percent. The shift was toward coming to view abortion as "wrong."

It is significant that we found widespread agreement on these aspects of public morality. And it is noteworthy that young adolescents seek to clarify their belief position on new issues.

Evidence of Erosion. The issue centers in the fact that the Adolescent-Parent data reflect a discernible shift in the adolescents' acceptance of some of the traditional moral beliefs. The three available to us from the survey relate to issues of national concern: drug use, sexual activity, and honesty. A decline occurs in the number of adolescents who regard the use of alcohol (Figure 12), premarital intercourse (Figure 13), and lying to parents (Figure 14) as wrong. Though their beliefs about the wrongness of shoplifting and racial discrimination remain continuously high, beliefs about the wrongness of activities that are of special concern to parents decline sharply from fifth to ninth grade. Take, for instance, the use of alcohol. The number of boys who view drinking beer as being wrong for them at their age drops from 76 percent for sixth-graders to 61 percent for ninth-graders; and the same relative decline in percentage occurs for the girls.

With respect to premarital relations, the number of boys who "don't think" they will have sexual intercourse before marriage drops from 50 percent for sixth-graders to 36 percent for ninth-graders. On this issue, the differences in response between boys and girls is one of the largest found in the study. The percent of girls who "don't think" they will have sexual intercourse before marriage remains high, with 61 percent of the ninth-graders maintaining this position.

With respect to lying, the great majority of early adolescents are agreed that lying to their parents is wrong. What is significant, however, is the erosion of this conviction (see Figure 14).

Though these changes in moral beliefs are obviously due to many factors, one can neither ignore the deliberate efforts of mass media to exploit the youth market nor the power of peer pressure to alter youth's moral convictions. David Rosenthal, writing in the *Rolling Stone Yearbook*,[6] sharply criticizes the "bad films aimed at 12-year-olds." His article takes the same position as that of Harry Haun in his article "Loss of Innocence

Figure 12. Belief About Drinking Alcohol*

Percent *wrong* or *very wrong*

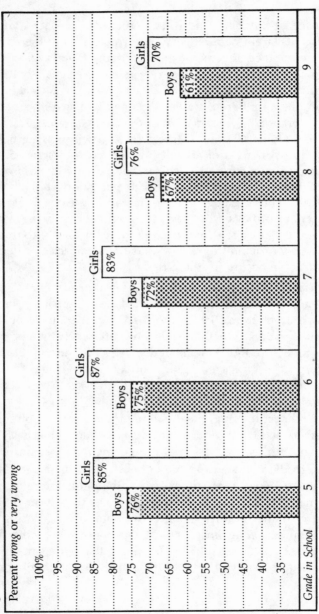

Grade in School

**Item:* "Jim is 13. Sometimes he and his friends get together and drink a couple of cans of beer. How right or wrong are they to do this?"

Figure 13. Percentage Opposed to Premarital Intercourse*

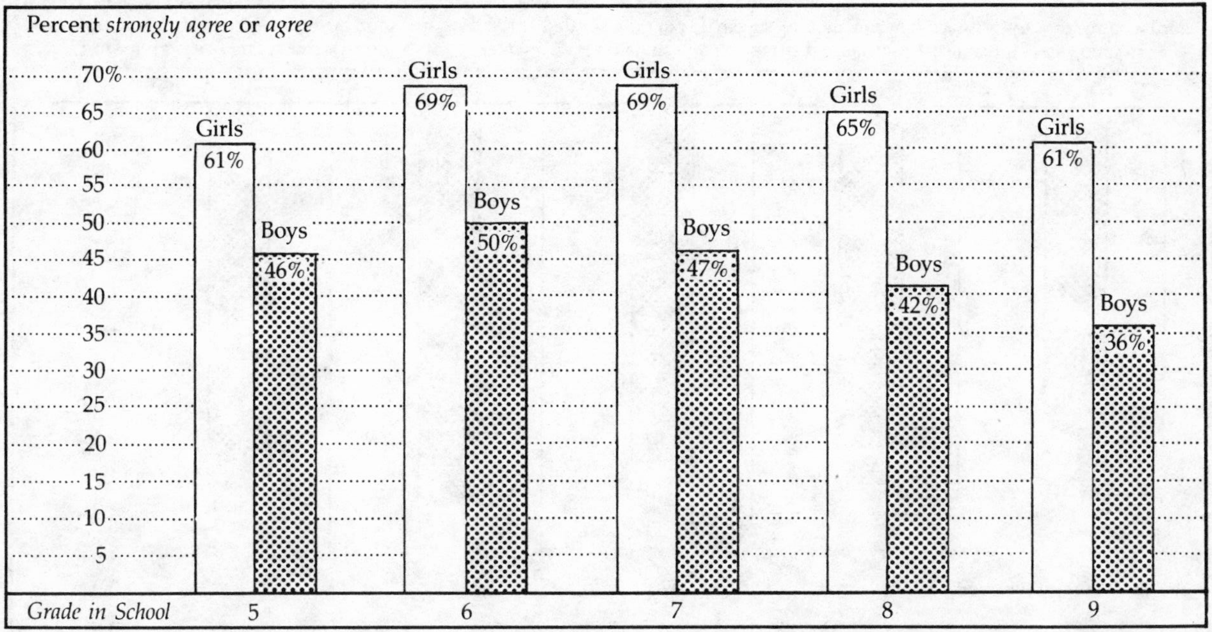

Percent strongly *agree* or *agree*

*Item: "I don't think I will have sexual intercourse (make love, "go all the way") with someone until I get married."

Figure 14. Belief About Lying to Parents*

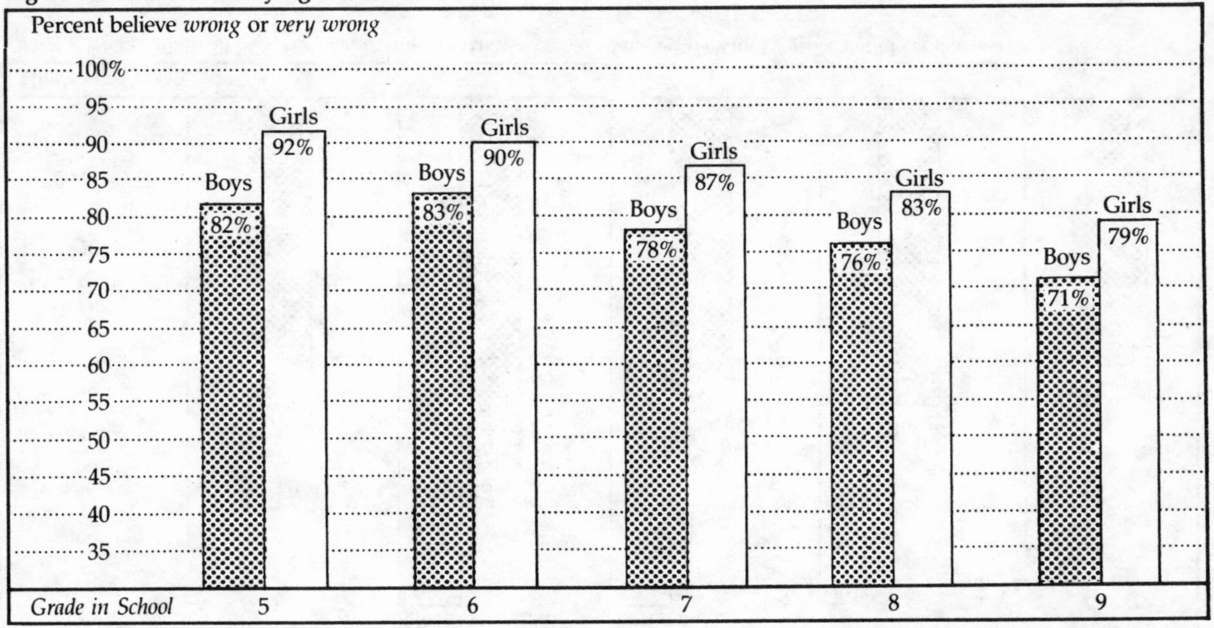

Percent believe *wrong* or *very wrong*

	5	6	7	8	9
Boys	82%	83%	78%	76%	71%
Girls	92%	90%	87%	83%	79%

Grade in School

*Item: "Gary is 12. His parents expect him to do his homework. Sometimes he lies to his parents and tells them he has done his homework when he really hasn't. He does this so that his parents won't keep asking him about his homework. How right or wrong is Gary to lie to his parents?"

Remains a Commercial Constant."[7] The concern of both writers is the sexploitation of the youth market.

Beer companies are using mass media to capture the youth alcohol market. Their unabashed effort to cultivate the youthful drinker has resulted in their being characterized by the Center for Science in the Public School as predators in "the business of creating drinkers." The use of sports heroes to promote the excitement and camaraderie of using alcoholic beverages can scarcely go unnoticed by highly vulnerable young adolescents.

Parents should be concerned over the values being presented through mass media. Our study of adolescents shows a strong relationship between exposure to mass media and the following: hedonism (seeing pleasure as the highest good); use of drugs and alcohol; sexually arousing activity; and rejection of traditional moral beliefs.

Evidence regarding this erosion of youth's moral beliefs and behavior came as a shock to representatives of Protestant denominations involved in the 1990 *Effective Christian Education* study. When the 300 representatives gathered in St. Louis to evaluate the survey findings on 11,000 of their youth and adults, they discovered that in the past year 54 percent of their high school juniors and seniors had been involved in three or more at-risk behaviors (e.g., binge drinking, sexual intercourse, thoughts of suicide). Any one of the 10 behaviors identified in the survey could sabotage a young person's future. Representatives learned that 42 percent of the boys and 46 percent of the girls claimed to have drunk to the point of intoxication at least once in the previous year.[8]

It is easy to see why the representatives of the six denominations each chose the findings on at-risk behaviors as being their highest concern.

Parental Concern. Voices are being raised today in protest of adults who don't expect young people to resist temptation.

William Raspberry, columnist for the *Washington Post,* wrote an article entitled, "It's Time for Black Adults to Make Teenage Virtue a Necessity."⁹ In addressing the alarming rise in pregnancies and child-bearing among unmarried teenagers (55 percent of all black children born in 1982 were born to a single mother), he quoted from a study by Harriet McAdoo. Though 80 percent of the teenagers recognized that having a baby was terribly disruptive to their educational and economic prospects, and half saw it as "ruining" their lives, 20 percent of the girls still expected to get pregnant and 44 percent of the boys expected they would get a girl pregnant. The conference where this study was reported toyed with the idea of introducing counter-incentives to getting pregnant. One proposal was to pay girls $200 every birthday as long as they avoid pregnancy and $2000 on their eighteenth birthday if they haven't gotten pregnant by then. Raspberry wrote:

> What fascinates and dismays me is how seldom the question of morality enters any of these discussions. That adolescents will be sexually active is taken as a given, and the only question seems to be how to avoid the natural consequences of that activity.
>
> I have the feeling that unless we get back to the old-fogey notion that teen-age sex is wrong (in the religious context, a sin) that morality demands the postponement of sexual activity, that virtue and decency are real concerns, the pragmatic approach is doomed to fail.

The 10,467 parents in the Adolescent-Parent study give top priority to the task of instilling moral beliefs in their children. Two out of three are much concerned about this task and wonder how best to carry out their responsibilities. They sense the conflict of values between their home and church on one hand, and society on the other. For that reason, when asked what help they would prefer, their top choice is "To help my child develop healthy concepts of right and wrong." A total of 70 percent say they are "very" or "quite" interested in programs that would equip them to give this help. The concern of over two-thirds of these parents is to instill in their children *a sense of morality* regarding what is right and wrong.

The need for greater attention to the issues is also being seen by professionals in the field of family counseling. Dolores Curran, in *Traits of a Healthy Family*,¹⁰ speaks of being pleasantly surprised to see how highly 551 professionals rated the traits "teaches a sense of right and wrong." These professionals, who touch families through their work in education, church, health, and family counseling or voluntary organizations, rank it number seven on a list of fifty-six possible characteristics of a healthy family. Strikingly, in a day when development of self takes precedence over the development of a moral life, these workers give priority to the teaching of morality.

Supportive Power of Moral Beliefs.   Parents can find encouragement in the fact that there is the potential in moral beliefs to provide inner strength and support to adolescents. We find that as acceptance of traditional moral standards or beliefs goes up for young adolescents, antisocial behaviors, drug and alcohol use, norm violations, and promiscuity go down.

This link between moral beliefs and behavior has appeared in several Search Institute studies. The most recent of these is the 1990 study of 47,000 students in 111 American communities, *The Troubled Journey.* Through a special analysis, Peter Benson found that youth who value sexual restraint are among the ones least likely to be involved in at-risk behaviors.[11] Additional evidence of this power of values and beliefs to influence behavior is strikingly apparent in a 1982 study of the religious beliefs and values of the 96th Congress by Peter Benson and Dorothy Williams of Search Institute.[12] From interviews (averaging thirty-five minutes in length) that include 72 percent of those drawn in an exact random sample, we gain unique information. We find that the beliefs and values of people in Congress are as good an indicator of their voting behavior as their party affiliation. When party affiliation and type of religious beliefs and values are combined, one can quite accurately predict how people in Congress will vote on matters such as defense, civil rights, humanitarian efforts, and foriegn aid.

For a parent, the implications of these findings are highly significant. It means that adolescents (as well as adults) who are helped to internalize moral beliefs and values, are likely to adopt behaviors compatible with these values.

A parent naturally wonders about the reliability of this kind of information. Therefore let us add that well over a hundred studies can be summoned to show a significant correlation between acceptance of traditional moral beliefs and moral restraint. Conversely, loss of traditional moral beliefs can be shown to be associated with a rise in immoral, illegal, and self-destructive behaviors.

In a separate study of data on youth ages fifteen to twenty-nine,[13] we analyzed what best predicts a young person's willingness to reject temptations such as alcohol abuse, swearing, premarital sexual intercourse, X-rated movies, and pornographic literature. We introduced thirty-nine different possibilities (variables) into the computer and let them compete with each other to see which variable best indicated a willingness to delay gratification. Interestingly, it was a moral belief that won out. Youth who believe that premarital sexual intercourse is "not permissible" are the ones most likely to show restraint in the many other behaviors related to moral behavior.

The Issue Involving a Sense of Moral Purpose

Our discussion now shifts to consideration of a higher expression of morality—feeling responsible for the needs of others. As was true for traditional moral beliefs, the majority of the young adolescents do accept a sense of responsibility for others. The Adolescent-Parent study gives clear evidences of a serving stance, particularly among the girls. Two out of three of the early adolescents speak of doing things for others. This is most encouraging.

Erosion of Moral Purpose. It is sobering to note that this sense of responsibility is not one that increases with age, but rather shows a decline from fifth to ninth grade. Take, for instance, the high concern fifth-graders show over hunger and poverty found in the United States. A total of 52 percent say they worry "very much" or "quite a bit" about this tragedy. It is something these fifth-graders are concerned about. But a steady decline appears in these percentages as the adolescents grow older. Only 31 percent of the ninth-graders identify this topic as a major concern. The same drop occurs in the value these young adolescents place on having a "world without war" (it ranks third in importance for fifth graders and eighth for ninth graders).

The critical issue is the apparent decline in a concern for people during these young adolescent years. A measure involving three items—adolescents' doing things that help people, wanting a world without war, and wanting a world without hunger or poverty—shows a discernible decline between the fifth and ninth grades (Figure 15). One might conclude from this and other changes that during early adolescence youth became increasingly self-oriented. The diminishing sense of moral purpose, however, centers primarily on boys, who appear to be less concerned with the needs of others.

Figure 16 suggests that girls differ from boys in their involvement in serving and helping activities. Not only are more of them involved in this way, but also there is a strong rise in the extent to which girls give aid to people in trouble, share money and food, give volunteer time to charities, and assist friends or neighbors. Girls are clearly more responsive to this aspect of a morality of responsibility than boys. The two issues we have identified emphasize the reason why parents in the Adolescent-Parent study need to give first priority to the teaching of healthy concepts of right and wrong. The challenge is to see that children become not only intelligent and healthy, but virtuous. As noted by Harvard psychiatrist Robert Coles,[14] parents need to inspire in their children a desire not only to get ahead and get along, but also to give to and help others. What children need as much as food, clothing, and a good education is moral purpose.

Adolescents need value judgments with which to critically evaluate the values and morality of the society in which they live. As parents we need to evaluate our own stand on controversial moral issues. By sharing them with our adolescents, we can help them learn to say "no" to unethical behaviors. Youth generally want this kind of direction-giving. Two young

Figure 15. Concern for People*

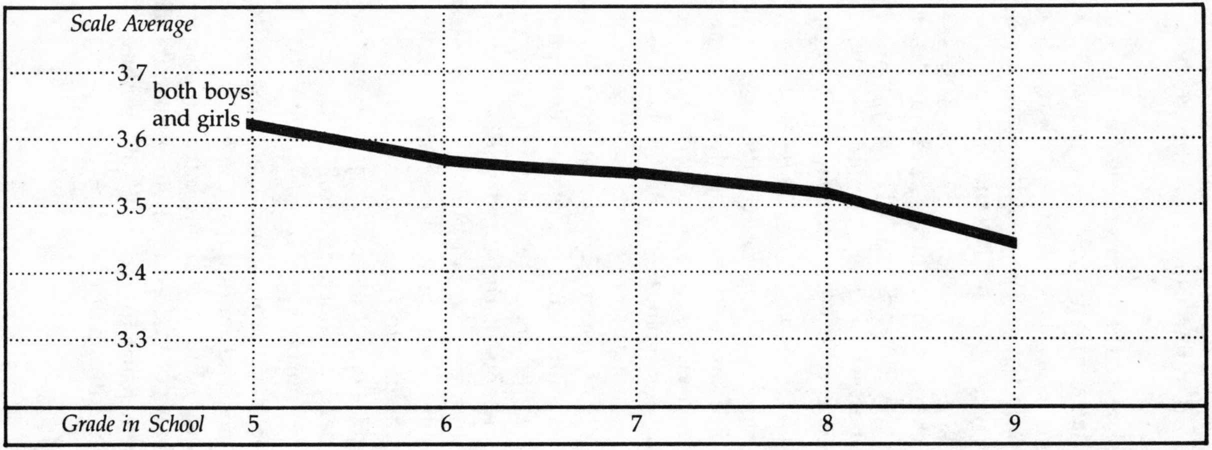

Scale Average

3.7
both boys
and girls
3.6
3.5
3.4
3.3

Grade in School   5   6   7   8   9

Item: "I worry about all the people who are hungry and poor in our country." Based on the average of three similar items

4 = Very much
3 = Quite a bit
2 = Somewhat
1 = Not at all

Figure 16. Prosocial Behavior*

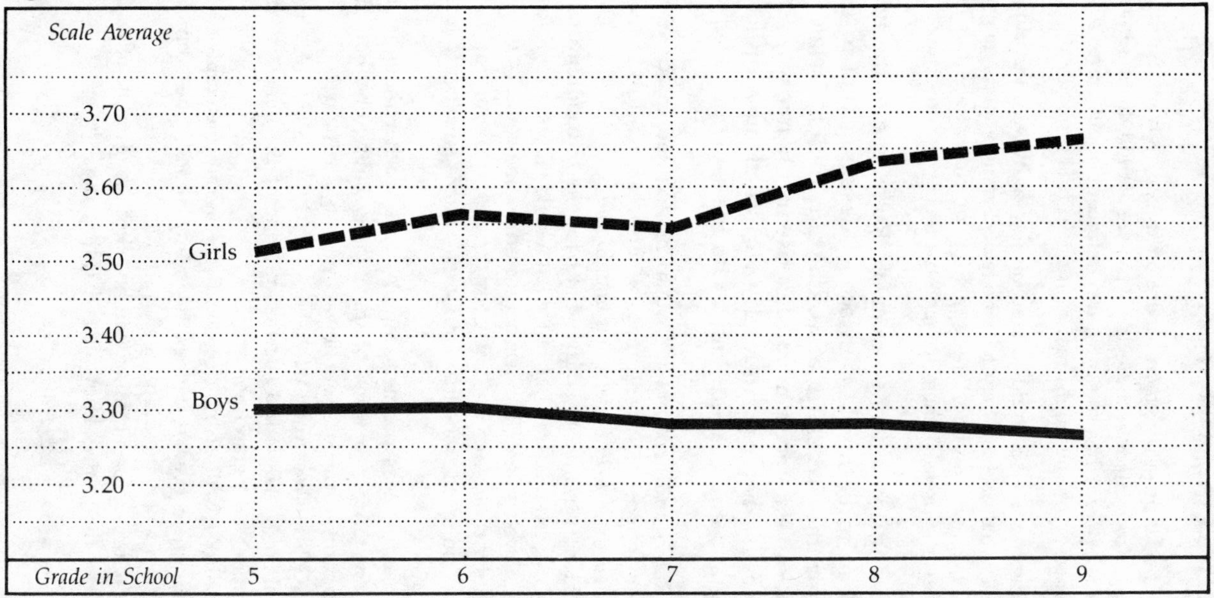

*The Prosocial Behavior scale is based on the average of six survey questions. The scale range is from 1 (low) to 5 (high).
Item: "How many hours did you give during the last month to help people outside the family (such as the poor, sick, aged, handicapped)?"

adults make their observations on this subject, based on experiences in their parental homes:

A parent should let us know when we are off track. It's true that most of the time we need freedom to decide what we should do in a given situation. But a parent has to warn an adolescent about some dangers. Otherwise he or she might realize it when it is too late.

I feel my parents were so afraid to step on our rights as individuals that they never told us how they felt about decisions or problems we had to face. I knew they had strong feelings or convictions but because they never expressed them it made me feel *alone* sometimes.

The following account of six-year-old Ruby, one of the first black children to be involved in school desegregation in the South during the sixties, is a striking illustration of how a young child can embrace a moral purpose in a heroic way. She did this because her parents took their stand on a difficult moral issue and encouraged Ruby to do the same.

Every day [Ruby] and another girl had to be escorted to school by federal marshals facing shouting mobs who threatened to kill them and who called them every vile name imaginable.

As a psychiatrist trained to study what happens to children under stress, Dr. Coles wanted to find out what would happen to Ruby's psychological development. The teacher admitted she couldn't understand how Ruby could take it. "She goes through hell every day and yet seems so composed," she told Dr. Coles. "She is so eager to learn and is such a nice child."

Dr. Coles said he was puzzled, too. When a teacher thought she observed Ruby talking to some of the people haranguing her, she asked her about it. It turned out she was praying for them.

When Dr. Coles asked Ruby why she was praying, she said it was "because I should." He found she was praying at the behest of her parents, minister, and grandmother.

"Do you think it will do much good?" she asked. Her reply: "We must pray for them even if it doesn't do any good." She admitted she prayed even when she didn't feel much like it.

She said she prayed because she had heard of the example of Jesus: "Father, forgive them, they know not what they do."

"That was her moral education," Dr. Coles said, noting that people come to develop some of the most admirable qualities in response to pain, suffering, and hardship.[15]

How Values and Beliefs Are Communicated

Moral actions develop from our moral beliefs. In other words, moral actions are the outcomes of the value orientation we hold. Our life priorities (values) and convictions (beliefs) are the soil out of which our actions emerge. Granted, there may be times when social pressures and stressful situations cause us to act out of emotion and without due restraint. But over time, our pattern of behavior is basically a reflection of our value orientation. This is true for us as parents and true also for our adolescent.

Sin as a Value Orientation

Where is the word "sin" in this picture? After all, sin figures prominently in both the Old and New Testaments. Does the concept of "sin" relate to the issue of one's value orientation? We believe that it does.

Sin can be defined as primarily a state of being, an orientation to life that centers on oneself, that places one's own interests in a position of top priority. That is why pride can be called the primary sin from which all others are derived. What we call unethical behavior or immoral acts are "sins" that result from the primary sin of self-interest or a self-centered value orientation. True, it is necessary for a parent to be concerned over behaviors or "sins" that are self-destructive (such as lying, stealing, drinking, vandalism, and fighting). They need to be restrained. But more important than these behaviors, and hence of greater potential concern to parents, is the value orientation out of which they arise.

It is not by chance that young adolescents involved in drug and alcohol use tend also to be involved in antisocial behaviors. These activities are highly intercorrelated.

The Adolescent-Parent study shows that associated with these activities are preferences for certain kinds of music, violence on television, and sexually arousing movies. The interlocking pattern of behaviors points to an underlying set of values that bring with it a tendency to reject the moral beliefs and standards that may be treasured by a parent. The Adolescent-Parent study shows a high correlation between youth whose pattern of behavior is as described above and those who reject traditional moral beliefs. The issue for us as parents is to help our children find the set of values that focuses on a moral purpose—a life contributing to the well-being of others, a life of significance.

If a child's orientation can be directed to a life of caring and concern for people—a life of moral purpose—the hoped-for positive behaviors will increasingly appear. On the other hand, the more a child's values center in self and personal gratification, the more he or she will show negative behaviors.

The Parents' Values

Values, a quality we can't see and certainly find difficult to define, are communicated most powerfully by parents. Though a child's friends may be influential, their power usually emerges as dominant only if the relationship of love and caring between parents is broken or vastly diminished. The prime communicator of values is still the parent.

When asked, "Whom do you enjoy more—your friends or your parents?" the answer is surprising. Sixty percent of the 8,165 adolescents say they enjoy both equally; 15 percent indicate a preference for their parents. The fact that no more than one in four prefer their friends suggests that for most adolescents a strong parent-child relationship exists along with their peer relationship.

The issue, then, is "What value orientation am I communicating to my child?" It is not enough to say that lying, cheating, and vandalism are wrong. These "sins" are simply expressions of a set of values that the child holds. The most important element of communication is the life direction a parent is giving the child through what he or she does and says.

One life direction or value orientation a parent can communicate is an approach of over-strictness that assumes that morality comes through controlling people by rules and regulations. It results in an authoritarian, restrictive approach to parenting and use of severe punishment. It tends to be unloving, unforgiving, and rigid. Though it may use the words of Scripture and orthodox Christianity, its spirit is poles apart from a Christianity of grace (unmerited love). Its focus is on external behaviors and the do's and don'ts of a personal morality.

Tragically, this well-intentioned and often earnest approach to parenting tends to drive children to do the very things that are forbidden. Our data consistently show that young people under such a regime seek out friends of contrasting standards and adopt behaviors that stand in defiance of their parents. Though they may not be able to put their feelings into words, they are repulsed by the relentless condemning spirit that lowers their self-esteem and causes them to battle with overwhelming feelings of guilt and no resolution of these emotions.

A contrasting value orientation is what Allen Keith-Lucas[16] calls a Christianity of Grace (meaning unmerited love). This stance focuses not on behaviors but on the underlying motivation of thankfulness for the love, the promise, and the presence of a living God. Parents with this value system know what it is to experience God's forgiveness and love themselves. In turn they can approach their children at a time of wrongdoing with an uncondemning spirit. If parents can give this value orientation to a child, they are giving a priceless gift. A sense of moral responsibility and concern for other people is a characteristic of this orientation.

An incident occurred in one of our studies that convinced us of how the values of respected adults are communicated to adolescents with whom they work. We were involved in a government-funded study that trained high school youth in friendship skills in order to reach out to lonely and alienated peers. The purpose of the study was to test the relative effectiveness of three different approaches to training these youth.

Because the project was government funded, care was used not to include any "God talk" or to sponsor any type of religious activity on its retreats. Likewise, when choosing the trainers of friendship skills, no thought was given to the value orientations of those selected—only to their skill and competence. By chance, one turned out to be an agnostic (a refugee from a moralistic background), the second a nominal member of a mainline denomination, and the third a psychotherapist who was also an ordained clergyman. Each person, highly skilled in human relations, developed a training program unique to his or her discipline. Each person, using the methodology unique to his or her specialization, taught friendship skills to a group of young adults, who in turn taught a group of high school students.

At three different times during the field experiment (beginning, middle, and end), a battery of forty-six scales or measures was given the high school youth. One of the questionnaires (an assessment of twenty-five scales) included measures of religious interest, participation, and belief. Though these three measures were not germane to the project, they were used because their items were intermingled with the others.

When comparing scores from the three training approaches, we were surprised to discover that changes had occurred in the religious interest and participation of the young people of two groups. There was a measurable drop in religious interest and involvement of youth being trained under the agnostic, and an increase for those trained under the ordained clergyman. Our best explanation for this unexpected change in scores on the religious measures was that these highly respected trainers had communicated a life direction and value orientation. Though they did not work directly with the high school youth, the power of their lives moved to them through the young adults. Their personalities were a contagion, particularly during retreats on weekends. This finding, confirmed by other studies, illustrates how values and beliefs are communicated when the authority figure is able to establish a congenial relationship. They are communicated by the modeling or lifestyle of a person as well as by verbal sharing. Values are primarily caught—not taught. They are unconsciously absorbed from those one loves and respects.

A strong incentive to moral living and a powerful inhibitor of living for the instant gratification of one's desires is found in the expectations of an adolescent's parents. Where love and respect is the common bond, the opinions and wishes of the parent carry considerable force. One young man, reminiscing on past behavior says, "What helped me decide against doing something I knew was wrong were the expectations of my folks. I respect and care for them and did not want to do something I knew would hurt them."

Working to Internalize Moral Beliefs

As parents we must know our position regarding what is right and wrong, and then be able to explain the reasonableness of this position. Such an approach to moral teaching is called induction. It relies on discussion and exploration, and in this process a child is helped to internalize a moral code. This method does not use compulsion or the common device of love withdrawal—"I won't like you if you do that." Rather, it attempts to explain why certain moral laws are important, that breaking them can violate some inner personal needs, and that breaking them can bring unhappiness to someone else as well. Induction appeals to a child's own internal resources for controlling and monitoring behavior. Over time, it creates internal standards an adolescent will use to control behavior.

The Adolescent-Parent study is conclusive regarding how a parent's behavior is tied with an adolescent's moral behavior.[17] Clearly, three parenting behaviors—demonstrative affection, authoritative (democratic) control, and inductive discussion—

are strongly tied with self-esteem, helping others, internalization of moral values, and a concern for people. Furthermore, when these parental approaches are used, one is less likely to find norm-breaking behavior, chemical use, and aggressive behaviors with one's adolescents. Granted, these parental behaviors do not assure moral behavior, because each adolescent makes his or her own decisions. But they do influence behavior.

Parents should also know that autocratic and permissive control, coercive discipline, and withdrawal of one's love consistently correlate with opposite behavior. Where parents use these approaches, one is more likely to find adolescents with low self-esteem, aggressive behaviors, chemical use, and a lack of interest in helping others.[8]

Parents who help their child to internalize moral beliefs that find their own focus on love of oneself, one's neighbor, and God gives the child an important source of strength. It equips the person to fight today's social epidemics. An adolescent can grow strong by resisting the pressures of an ethic of "I want" and adopting the ethic of what is helpful to both self and others.

6. Cry for a Shared Faith

Each morning I saw my father take his Bible and go into his study for private devotions. I felt that if it was important for him as a grown-up, it must be for me, too.

—COLLEGE STUDENT

"Do we have family devotions?" Janet repeated the question after her interviewer. Then she looked over at her husband Bob and they exchanged a helpless laugh.

"I haven't heard that word for a long time," said the husband. "We had it when I was a kid."

"Don't you remember, Bob," said his wife, "we started out having something like that when the children were small?"

"Yeah, we were idealists, then, I guess."

"There are problems, aren't there?" The interviewer was tentative, waiting for a response.

"You bet there are," said Bob. "The last years I've traveled a lot in my business—days at a time, so Janet is alone with the kids."

Jane chimed in quickly. "I work part-time now, and when I get home, I'm a chauffeur. First I bring Betty to her cheerleader's practice—it's every day after school, you know. John's in cub football now and then he'll start hockey. There's no time for *anything*, let alone something structured like family devotions. We scarcely eat together. I'm a short-order cook."

Bob was a bit meditative. "I can see where it would be a good thing. I hardly know what my kids are thinking anymore. But," and he gave that helpless little laugh again, "time is the problem. Time."

Some readers may find such expressions as "private devotions," and "family devotions" archaic. What meaning do they have for today's parent or today's adolescent? Aren't they merely throwbacks to an earlier age?

The desire for a shared faith is only a muted cry. Though religious faith ranks high in importance for parents in the Adolescent-Parent study, it is seldom a topic of discussion in the home. This chapter is called "The Cry of Shared Faith" because 68 percent of the parents do express interest—"very much" or "quite a bit"—in learning "how to help my child grow in religious faith." There is a longing expressed here. The cry is a real one.

The purpose of this chapter is to draw attention to the critical need for parental sharing of faith within the family. The chapter considers four topics:

- The issue of sharing faith
- What faith can mean to an adolescent
- Why sharing faith is needed in a family
- How faith is shared

The Issue of Sharing Faith

In the Judeo-Christian tradition, the command to teach one's children about God goes far back in the life of God's people. When Moses, the leader of the Israelites and giver of the Ten Commandments, spoke to his people about entering the Promised Land, he told them they were to keep alive the story of how God had led them out of slavery in Egypt. They were to tell of how God promised to bless his people. Moses' instructions were clear: They were to teach these commands and promises to their children *at home*. How were they to accomplish this? Through conversation, symbol, and ritual.

You shall therefore lay up these words of mine in your heart and in your soul, and you shall bind them as a sign upon your hand, and you shall teach them to your children, talking of them when you are sitting in your house, and when you are walking by the way, and when you lie down, and when you rise. And you shall write them upon the doorposts of your house and upon your gates, that your days and the days of your children may be multiplied in the land. . . . (Deuteronomy 11:18–21)

Faithfully, devout parents through the centuries have followed these very commands—using different methods, perhaps, but keeping the theme of what God has done for them and how he continues to show his power and love.

A teenager of today speaks of how this kind of teaching was used in her home:

We learned about God chiefly through Bible stories in our family devotions and at night before we went to bed. When I have a family of my own, I would want to do the same thing. I love Bible stories, and I can remember them well from when I was a little girl.

In 1982, 551 professional counselors and educators were given a list of fifty-six traits characterizing a healthy family. They were told to rate them in order of importance. In the resulting book, *Traits of a Healthy Family*, author Dolores Curran reports that the trait "a shared religious core" ranked number 10.[1] Similarly, when Hamilton McCubbin studied the effects of war on the families of men who were killed, missing, or prisoners in Vietnam, he found that families were more resilient if they had strong religious beliefs.[2]

One would expect parents in the Adolescent-Parent study to be discussing their faith at home. When ranking sixteen values, they give fourth place to "having God at the center of my life." This is outranked only by their desire to have a happy family life, to be a good parent, and to have wisdom. Six in ten of these parents attend church once a week or more, two in three pray most days or every day, and one in two report being active in their church (See Figure 17). Thus it's not surprising that such a high value is placed on God-centeredness. When these 10,467 parents were asked, "Over all, how important is religion in your life?" the overwhelming majority—80 percent of the mothers and 67 percent of the fathers—affirmed that "it is the most" or at least "one of the most important influences in my life."

Figure 17. Specific Religious Behaviors of Parents

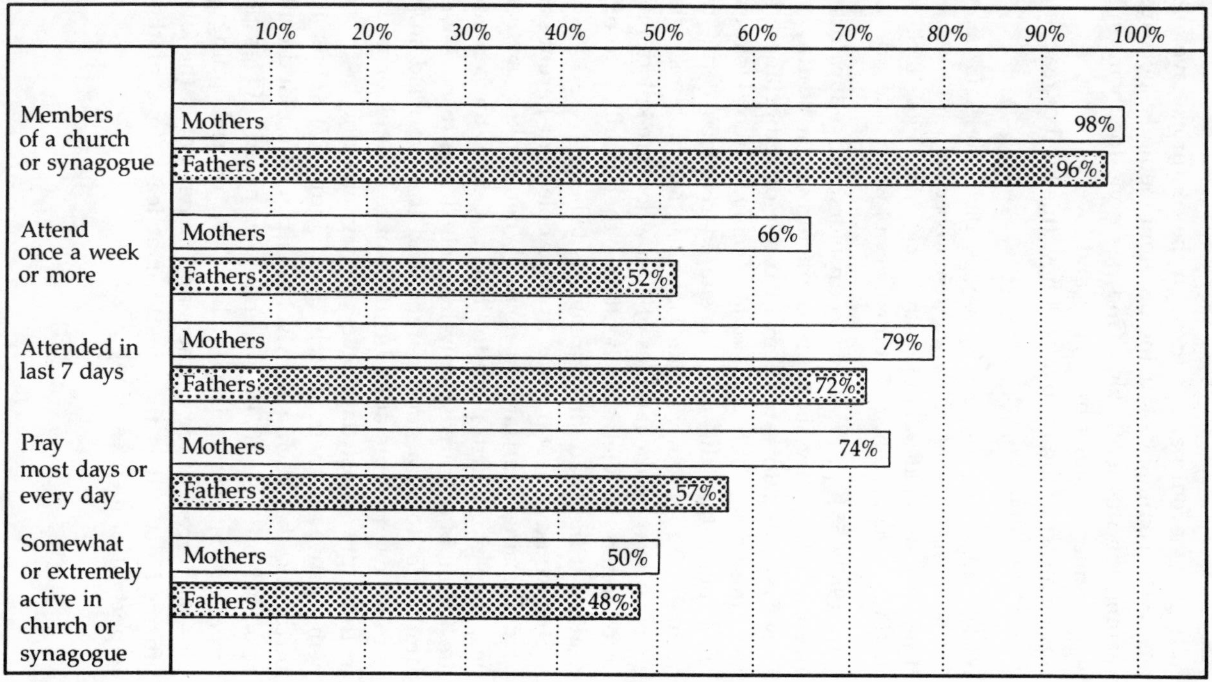

	10%	20%	30%	40%	50%	60%	70%	80%	90%	100%

Members of a church or synagogue
- Mothers: 98%
- Fathers: 96%

Attend once a week or more
- Mothers: 66%
- Fathers: 52%

Attended in last 7 days
- Mothers: 79%
- Fathers: 72%

Pray most days or every day
- Mothers: 74%
- Fathers: 57%

Somewhat or extremely active in church or synagogue
- Mothers: 50%
- Fathers: 48%

Table 6. Importance of Religion to Parents

Response	Percentage Mother	Percentage Father
It is the most important influence in my life	36%	26%
One of the most important	44	41
Somewhat important	18	26
One of the least important	2	6
The least important	0	2

Do their adolescent children rate the religious interest of their parents similarly? Interestingly, yes. When asked to rate "How important do you think religion is in your mother's/father's life?" their ratings agree fairly well with their parents' rating. Ratings of mothers do not differ on the average more than 5 percent. Fathers were not as easy to judge; this shows up with an average discrepancy rating of 9 percent. One-fourth of the adolescents assumed that a religious faith was not important to their father.

Adolescents in the study share the personal conviction of their parents about the importance of religion.

A majority of the young adolescents say it is the most important or one of the most important influences in their lives (See Table 7).

Table 7. Importance of Religion to Youth

Response	Grade in School				
	5	6	7	8	9
The most important influence					
Boys	29%	23%	17%	18%	17%
Girls	27	25	20	17	20
One of the most important influences					
Boys	31%	31%	32%	31%	29%
Girls	33	32	35	38	35

The enigma, however, is this: though religion is identified as important by both parents and adolescents, it is almost a taboo subject in the home. When asked, "How often does your family sit down together and talk about God, the Bible

. . . or other religious things?" 42 percent of the young adolescents say this never happens; 32 percent say this topic is discussed once or twice a month, 13 percent say it is discussed once a week. And this, it must be noted, is the finding from a survey of largely church-connected families, of whom 97 percent are members of a church.

This finding is supported by other studies. A 1980 study of Lutherans showed that only 8 percent of the families surveyed maintain a practice of discussing their faith or praying together as a family.[3] These low percentages of active sharing in the home are part of a larger national trend. Gallup's 1980 poll of Americans showed a decline in the proportion wanting their children to have religious training, a decline that has been in process since the mid-1960s.[4] The seriousness of these findings was again underscored by the 1990 *Effective Christian Education* study. Through careful measure of mature faith indicators, the results showed that two-thirds of Protestant young people have an undeveloped faith.

Parents who talk often about faith in the home double the probability that their youth will be involved in the life of the church, reflect a faith intentionality, and be service-oriented. In this study, however, two-thirds (64%) of church youth in 1990, as contrasted with 42% in 1980, report never or rarely having anything resembling family devotions.[5]

Why has there been such a decline in home conversations about matters of faith?

One answer might be that the fruits of declining instruction in faith in the mid-1960s are now appearing. Parents who have received scant biblical training and little opportunity to verbalize what they do believe, feel inadequate to teach at home. They reason that if their child should begin to question them and they do not know the answer, it would be humiliating and confusing.

As illustrated at the beginning of this chapter, there are homes today, in which there may be very good intentions of having a "Christian home," complete with talks about one's faith. Attempts may have been made when children were young, but as they near adolescence, the family begins to fragment: social life and work obligations become more complex; children begin participating in extracurricular activities and working at part-time jobs. A meal is scarcely ever eaten when everyone is together; if the family is together, someone is watching a TV program at the same time. "How can we even have time to talk about such things?" parents cry out. "We know we should, but it's impossible!"

Some parents regard church and confirmation instruction as the proper and only place for religious training. It is argued that pastors and their lay assistants are the only qualified teachers of religion.

Still another reason might be that there is no agreement between parents concerning matters of faith. One parent may be interested; the other may not, or may be of another faith. So, for the sake of harmony, this subject is omitted from discussion in the home. Some parents find it impossible to communicate their faith to their children, because it is not real for the parents themselves.

Parents' desire to learn. Though religious discussions are rare, most parents of the 10,467 wish it were different. When asked in the Adolescent-Parent study about training programs that a school, agency, or church might provide, strong interest is expressed in several possible subjects. The top two were the programs described in Table 8.

Furthermore, parents in the survey were asked if they wished they could talk more with their children about "God and other

Table 8. Preference of Training Programs for Children

Subject	Percent "Very" or "Quite" Interested
How to help a child develop healthy concepts of right and wrong	70%
How to help a child grow in religious faith	68%

religious topics." As shown in Table 9, 40 percent of the mothers and 28 percent of the fathers said "definitely."

Table 9. Desire to Talk More

Response	Percentage Mother	Percentage Father
Would like to talk more about God and other religious topics		
Definitely	40%	28%
Probably	47	47
Not sure	8	15
Probably not	5	1
Definitely not	1	1

The reluctant dragon in this area seems to be father. Nevertheless, a significant proportion of both parents "definitely" want more conversations about religious issues, and an additional 47 percent "probably" do. The cry for greater sharing is clear: almost four out of five are interested. It is highly significant that fewer than one-fifth of the parents resist this subject.

What most parents do not realize is that a mature religious faith has resident power to create what they want their children to be, namely, caring, other-centered people.

What Faith Can Mean to an Adolescent

Religion is largely ignored in most books on adolescent development. It is a dimension few research psychologists consider when trying to understand the adolescent. Hence little has been known about the importance of a religious faith in the life of an adolescent.

This study of 8,165 young adolescents does give information regarding their religious faith and provides evidence as to its possible impact in their lives. Four measures of religious perception were used for both adolescents and parents. These perceptions are described below.

Four Religious Perceptions

Variety appears in the religious perceptions of young adolescents and their parents. By reflecting on the following themes or emphases developed by Peter Benson of Search Institute,[6] parents may sense which theme best characterizes their adolescents.

1. *Liberating religion* is experienced as freeing and enabling. People for whom religion is liberating tend to place a good deal of emphasis on the fact that God accepts them just as they are and that salvation is a gift, not something earned. It is an orientation sometimes referred to as a "Gospel" orientation, as opposed to a "Law" orientation.

2. *Restricting religion* is experienced as stressing limits, controls, guidelines, and discipline. Whereas liberating religion stresses freedom, restricting religion emphasizes limits.

3. *Vertical orientation* has to do with how one interprets one's responsibility as a person of faith. Those with a vertical orientation (later referred to as Centrality of Religion) tend to see that the believer's priorities should be to establish and maintain a close relationship to God. The emphasis is on prayer, worship, and other activities that keep one's focus on God.

4. *Horizontal orientation* is typically an emphasis on themes of love and justice, and those with a horizontal orientation tend to reach out and care for others.

Our measures of each theme show that young adolescents in this study tend to experience religion more as liberating than restricting. In part, this means that young adolescents focus more on God's love than on God as judge or rule-giver. Most adolescents in this study affirm that religious responsibility includes a horizontal commitment—reaching out to help others. Finally, three of the scales discussed in this chapter—religious centrality, liberating religion, horizontal orientation—are tied to desirable values and good patterns of behavior.

Behaviors Associated With Each Perception

The Adolescent-Parent study gives clear indications that moral behaviors, service activities, and the avoidance of self-destructive practices tend to be found among religious adolescents. Specifically, where religious faith is central and important, one is more likely to find helping and serving adolescents. Such youth are more likely to have high self-esteem and a positive attitude toward church. They are also more likely to refrain from drug and alcohol use.

Adolescents characterized by a liberating faith will not only evidence the behavior indicated above, but also will be less racially prejudiced and less likely to be involved in antisocial activities such as fighting, vandalism, shoplifting, cheating at school, or lying to parents (see Table 10).

Where a horizontal religion's emphasis is strong, one is likely

**Table 10. How Religious Orientations Correlate
With Attitudes and Behaviors***

Youth's Values, Motivations, Identity	Liberating	Horizontal	Restricting
Self-esteem	+		−
Moral internalization	+	+	−
Acceptance of traditional standards	+	+	
Achievement motivation	+	+	−
Ageism	−		
Sexism			+
Racial prejudice	−		+
Positive attitude toward church	+	+	
Value world peace			
Youth's Behaviors			
Prosocial behavior	+	+	−
Drug and alcohol use	−		+
Antisocial behavior	−		+

* + means that the higher the religious orientation, the more likely that the other variable is high.

− means that the higher the religious orientation, the more likely that the other variable is low.

(Correlations range from .12 to .38 and are statistically significant.)

to find young adolescents who place a high value on world peace and show a value orientation that emphasizes concern for people.

By way of contrast, adolescents who view religion as restricting are linked to a number of undesirable characteristics. Those high on this measure tend to be high on antisocial behaviors and alcohol use. They are linked also to racial prejudice and sexism. Among these adolescents who feel tied down by religion one can also expect to find low self-esteem, failure to internalize moral standards, and a lower achievement drive.

This highly significant measure of religion shows that a misperceived religion—one focused on standards and prohibitions—can have a negative effect. Its impact is similar to that of an autocratic approach to parenting.

Why Sharing Faith Is Needed in a Family

Why should parents break the silence and initiate conversations about spiritual or religious issues? There are three compelling reasons: religious doubt, decline in religious interest, and the relationship between religious faith and style of parental discipline.

Religious Doubt

One reason for bringing discussion into the home relates to the emergence of religious doubt during adolescence. The percentages who attribute some truth to the statement "I'm not sure what I believe about God" are indicated in Table 11.

Table 11. Youth Who Attribute Some Truth to Statement of Doubt

Response		*Grade in School*				
		5	6	7	8	9
I'm not sure what I believe about God.						
	Boys	45%	46%	51%	55%	62%
	Girls	42	46	52	53	54

For boys as well as girls, the percentage who are unsure of what they believe about God increases with grade in school. This increase is accompanied by a sharp decline in the percentage who claim that religion is "the most important influence in my life." These measures indicate a possible erosion in the faith that many parents highly prize for their children.

For over twenty-five years we had groups of youth in our home to discuss issues in the light of Scripture. Many years after they had been members of a group, we invited them back to our home to tell us what they remembered and what they especially appreciated. We learned that what youth expressed at the time when they were teenagers held true in their memories years later. "I appreciated being able to speak openly of my doubts and differing ideas and not be immediately jumped on and told, 'You mustn't talk like that,'" said one young adult. Another said, "I was confused in my beliefs as a teenager and said some rather blasphemous things, but the group cared enough to hear me out, and because of their acceptance and understanding, I am a believer today in Christ and his Word."

The issue of doubt can actually become a plus in conversations about faith. Usually an adolescent's doubts are rooted in a need for answers. Opportunities to probe, make distinctions, examine, and scrutinize actually further a function of doubt encouraged in the New Testament. Doubt can be a state of openmindedness in which faith is asking the intellect for help.

Relation of Belief to Faith. Beliefs are not the same as faith. In her book *To Set One's Heart,*[7] Sara Little expresses this in an interesting way. She says that beliefs are components of faith. They might be described as "inferences about what is going on within a person" as it pertains to one's relationship to a personal, loving, redeeming God. The struggle, then, is to *understand* those inner realities and *verbalize* them. Beliefs take form when faith "asks the intellect for help" in explaining what one has experienced. In *saying* the words of faith we clarify our understanding of relationship to God. One reason it is hard to discuss faith issues at home is that neither parents nor children have struggled to verbalize the words of faith—in other words, their *beliefs*. We need informal and structured discussions about matters of faith in order to clarify this for ourselves and each other. As noted earlier, putting concepts into words is difficult for some boys, in particular.

Parents who have trouble verbalizing their faith would do well to seek help in this area themselves. The built-in sharing during adult Bible discussions, for instance, can make a great deal of difference. This was the case for David, who himself had grown up in a largely nonverbal family. His children remember him as "the silent one" during their adolescence. A small-group Bible study at church, however, has helped him verbalize his faith. Today communication between David and his grandchildren is a heartwarming thing to see.

Decline in Religious Interest

The Adolescent-Parent study shows a marked decline for religious interest during adolescence, which usually finds its lowest point with ninth-grade boys. A striking portrayal of this decline is seen in an eight-item measure of the centrality religion holds in the life of an adolescent. From seventh grade on, the average scores drop each year for boys, indicating a growing alienation from the faith of their childhood years (see Figure 18).

This decline is matched by a changing attitude toward the church. Here again, the interest of fifth-graders represents a high point that steadily erodes to ninth grade (see Table 12).

Table 12. Youth Attitudes Toward the Church

Response		Grade in School				
		5	6	7	8	9
How important is	Boys	54%	49%	45%	42%	40%
your church or	Girls	58	53	49	48	51
synagogue to you?*	Total	56	51	47	45	46

*Percent "very important" or "extremely important."

Figure 18. Centrality of Religion*

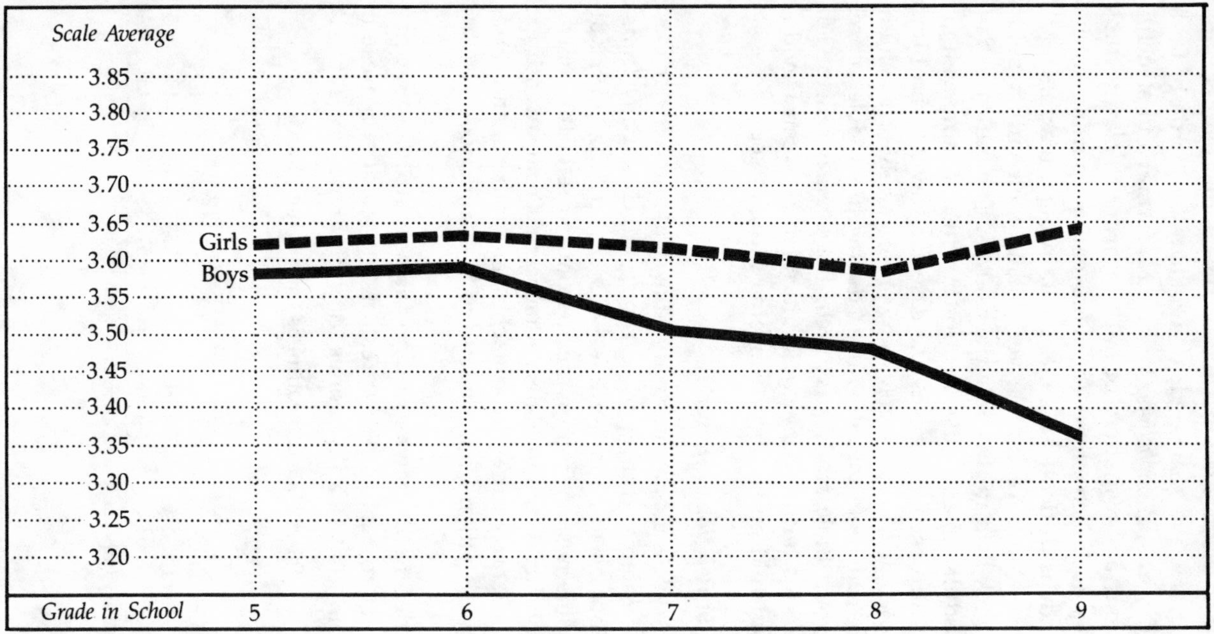

*Centrality of Religion scale is based on the average of eight items. The scale range is from 1 (low) to 5 (high).
Item: "Overall, how important is religion in your life?"

These indices of religious interest are paralleled by answers to two direct questions: "How much do you want God at the center of your life?" and, "How much do you want to be a part of a church?"

The answers are revealing. There is a steady decline until the eighth grade in adolescents' desire to have God as central in their lives or to be a part of a church or synagogue (see Figure 19).

What accounts for this erosion of interest? There is no reason to attribute the decline merely to characteristics of adolescence. On the contrary, there is reason to anticipate a rise instead of a fall. Why? Adolescence is a time of unfolding, which historically has been identified with religious conversion or commitment. The studies of Starbuck in 1899, replicated thirty years later by E. J. Clark, identify the ages of twelve and sixteen as times of religious awakening or conversion to the faith.[8]

This decline of interest may be due to neglect with respect to the historic functions of the father as religious leader in the home; or it may be because this age group is neglected in the life of the church. In most denominations, these youth are regarded as being too old for Sunday school and too young for the high school youth program.

Another possible explanation for decline of interest is youth's vulnerability, or susceptibility to temptation. During this age, which has been identified as one of greatest vulnerability, adolescents are being exposed to powerful media presentations that teach a contrasting value system. This exposure is significant. One-half (51 percent) of the adolescents in the Adolescent-Parent survey say that on an average school day they watch TV three hours or more.

In spite of mass media and peer pressures, one need not assume that youth's interest in matters of faith must decline as they advance toward their senior year in high school. Though this decline typifies most youth of Protestant denominations, it is not true for adolescents of the Southern Baptist Convention. The percentage of their youth who show an integrated faith *mounts* sharply from seventh to twelfth grade. This striking

Figure 19. Value Placed on God and Church*

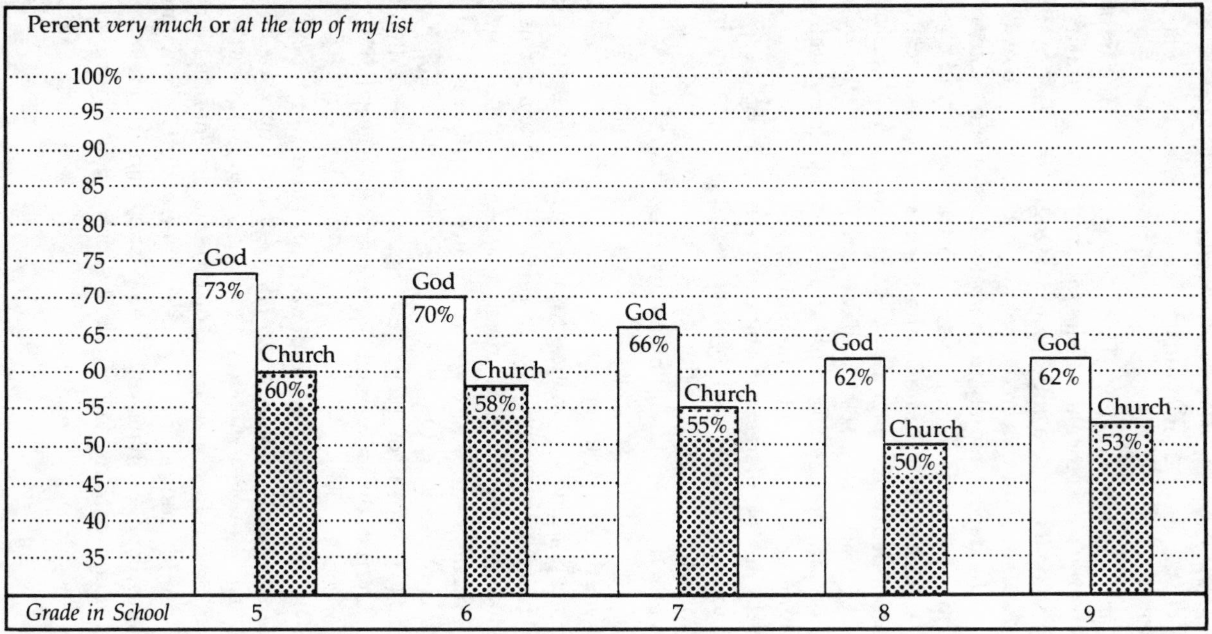

Percent *very much* or *at the top of my list*

God 73%	God 70%	God 66%	God 62%	God 62%
Church 60%	Church 58%	Church 55%	Church 50%	Church 53%

Grade in School: 5, 6, 7, 8, 9

*Item: "How much do you want 'to have God at the center of my life'?"
*Item: "How much do you want 'to be part of a church or synagogue'?"

contrast means that a ministry in home and congregation can reverse the trend that is pressed on youth by today's societal values.[9]

Whatever the reason for the decline of religious interest in youth, we as parents need to initiate ways of reversing the downward trend if we do not wish to see our children dissociate themselves completely from the religious resource of the family.

Religious Faith and Style of Parental Discipline

A third compelling reason for becoming attentive to the business of sharing faith as a family is related to the issue of how parents discipline their children. As indicated in the previous chapter, almost half the parents in the Adolescent-Parent study take a moralistic stance toward Christianity. Their orientation is toward rules and regulations. The statement "I believe that God has a lot of rules about how people should live their lives" was agreed with by 52 percent; and 41 percent agreed "I believe God is very strict."

A consistent finding here and in other studies carried out by Search Institute is that adolescents raised under an autocratic style of control are less likely to experience religion as a liberating power. On the contrary, they are likely to see it as restricting. If adolescents see it in this way, their obvious reaction is to move away from religion. This is precisely what boys in the sample are doing. As was shown in Figure 18, religion and the church are becoming less and less prominent in their lives.

Parents should know that a caring stance of parental nurturance and democratic (authoritative) control both correlate with a liberating, challenging, and people-oriented (horizontal) faith. Ranking a close second in encouraging a living, action-oriented faith are the two other dimensions found in a democratic (authoritative) approach, namely, trust by parents and family closeness. In other words, if we as parents engender a caring, affectionate, trusting atmosphere in the home, our adolescents will not be trying to escape. Instead, they will be likely to accept our beliefs and values.

How Faith Is Shared

This chapter has led from the question of the what and the why of shared faith to the critical climax—how it is done. Faith is shared in family life in three ways: (1) during daily interaction, (2) during structured times of worship, and (3) by "doing the truth together."

Faith Is Shared in the Natural Flow of Home Life. In Deuteronomy 11:19, the writer says, "You shall talk about these things when you are sitting in your house and when you are walking by the way, and when you lie down and when you rise." Here our attention is drawn to the fact that the focus of Scripture is on daily life; the Word gives us divine insight, which reorganizes our whole perspective on life. This experience of sharing the faith as a natural flow of home life does typify some families.

Several young adults we interviewed speak of the atmosphere in their parental home as being open to talking about God in the ordinary routines of life. In fact, as one young man put it, "It happens all the time. There's no specific point when we say, 'Now, let's talk about God.' "

A teenager who was a dinner guest in such a home remarked afterwards, "They were talking about just ordinary things, and all of a sudden you realized they were involved in a theological discussion." When questioned further as to her interpretation of "theological," she described it as, "Oh, you know, how something related to a Christian view of things. It was interesting to see that everyone was talking, not just the parents."

These are the homes in which children "pick up" on religion as being important to their parents. They feel free to ask questions themselves and venture opinions. As one young woman from such a home expressed it, "For my mother, when

I was growing up, there were no unaskable questions about faith.''

Fifty-one percent of all adolescents in the Adolescent-Parent study expressed much interest in receiving more help on what it means to be a Christian. Young people of this age, struggling for identity, warm to the freedom of expressing doubts and asking questions without feeling stupid, getting hurt, or being put down. They like the freedom to debate with people who have an opposite opinion. It is a way to arrive at a personal belief and know why.

When young people learn that parents are committed to open discussion carried on in a spirit of humility, they will grow in their ability to share personal experiences and ideas. It is in this kind of atmosphere also that the strength of a parent's faith comes through to a child, as, for instance, in a time of great stress.

A young woman remembers, "I was a teenager when my brother was killed in a plane crash. The witness of my parents' faith during that time was a pervasive one." Sharing beliefs may mean sharing together deep hurts and pain so that healing may come to the whole family. Parents need not fear showing hurts to their children.

Another young adult tells of the death of a teenage brother who was close to her in age. Her father, an ardent Christian, appeared through the whole experience always "radiant and strong," even though he deeply loved his son.

I used to wonder how he could be that way—kind of superhuman, while I was often bitter and resentful. Then one day, after my brother had been dead for some months, I happened to walk by the room where my dad was taking a shower. I realized he was sobbing loudly, and I heard him shouting out to God, "Why? Why? Why did you take him from me?"

Something happened inside of me that day. I felt so bad for my dad, but I felt warm and released, too. My dad couldn't understand "why?" either. He was human, too.

Unplanned conversations may become counseling times. Our

study shows that adolescents are often eager to discuss problems concerning their friends. But sometimes the problem comes closer to home—when the young person in the family is the one who needs help, and comes with a confession. At such times parents may struggle with a sense of disappointment or shock at what is confessed. Our emotions may make it hard to continue the conversation in the same open manner as before. But it is exactly at this point that our child needs us most.

Disappointment in another person, failure, anger, shame, illness—all are unplanned circumstances, but they demand that families talk about them. Vocational goals, losing a job, good grades and bad grades—these represent the endless flow that is woven into the warp and woof and faith of a family. If parents talk about them together with children, pray about them, and even cry about them if need be, family members are reaching out together for the hand of God.

A friend says, "We have shared bad financial reverses, my husband nearly died in a terrible accident, we have lived many years with a child who is ill with a fatal disease. But through it all my husband and I are thankful for the faith that has sustained all of us and brought us closer together."

This openness also makes it possible to laugh together. By laughing we do not mean getting sarcastic delight from another's discomfort, or giving flip answers to another's seriousness. Rather, we are referring to the ability to laugh at "the fool" in oneself. If members of a family are able to do this, they will be able to see humor in countless everyday situations and share them with each other.

There is a deeper sense in which use of humor is a freeing experience: when persons can see the comic side of a painful, frustrating, or hurtful situation. They see it because they can see "the fools" in themselves and others. When one can no longer laugh at the difficulties of life, one is cutting off a source of God-given freedom, one which parents can give as a heritage to their children. An old Jewish proverb expresses it thus:

There are three things which are real: God, human folly, and laughter. The first two are beyond our comprehension so we must do what we can with the third.

A sense of humor is a "saving grace," as one family member described it—a gift of God to be enjoyed in the context of our lives as God's children.[10]

The natural flow of life may be full of beautiful and laughing times. But there may be ugly times, too, when tempers flare and words are said that can never be recalled. The glory of shared faith lies in the stumbling words of forgiveness—sometimes hard to come by—between father and son, brother and sister, mother and daughter.

The open home, the place where friends and relatives can come and go, talk and eat together—that is part of the natural flow, too. Karen Mains, in *Open Heart, Open Home*, says of these times, in her own girlhood experience, "Food on family occasions . . . was sharing, a communal expression. There was not much emphasis on elegance or finery, but a high priority on how hot the verbal debates could wax, how riotous the laughter would rage, how deeply the discussions would range." During such times, she adds, "We shared life and being."[11] We noted as Bible discussion leaders for our youth group that when we had several potluck suppers in a row, sharing of self and faith became a much more natural process.

Faith Is Also Shared During Structured Times. Within the family, it means believing "This is an important part of our life together." From Old Testament times, devout Jews and Christians have continued some form of family "worship." People who have seen *Fiddler on the Roof* on film or on stage, for example, will have vivid memories of Sabbath worship in the home of Tevye and Golda. Recently, we participated in a Passover meal (family Seder) and were reminded again of the sense of celebration the family experiences in this ritual, and the repetitive beauty of saying together, "Blessed art thou, O Lord our God, King of the Universe, Who has kept us in life, Who has preserved us and has enabled us to reach this season."

Granted, in the pioneer days of our land, family devotions may not have had much beauty or drama about them; in fact, they may have been very prosaic. But if done in an atmosphere of love, they were still remembered fondly.

Such was the case with Uncle Clarence Strommen, now ninety years of age, who clearly remembers family devotions in the farm home when he was a teenager:

I remember my father and mother gathering us children for family devotions after chores and supper. Pa had been a heavy drinker who had sometimes treated us pretty bad when he was drunk. But after he became a Christian, when I was about twelve, he really changed. No, he never preached, he never said anything in church, but it was in our *home* we saw the change. It was like he had said to himself, "From now on, we will have devotions every day."

Even though he did not verbalize the thought, perhaps Uncle Clarence's Pa sensed that this might be his most lasting memorial and witness to his children.

I (Irene) remember my own family a generation later, in the 1930s. Saturday morning after breakfast was "special devotions time" for us. Each child in the family took turns reading the Bible story and was given the privilege of asking questions of everyone else. And while the emphasis of my parents was on free prayer, every once in a while my father would say, "Today you may read the prayer of the church." And so, ingrained in us also would be prayers for the government and for leaders of church and state, a wide scope that went way beyond our little world. We also had a favorite one-stanza hymn we often sang; then we prayed the benediction together. These are powerful memories even today. I remember that my younger sister was sometimes reluctant to come inside from play. Occasionally, my father would say, "Let her play." He remembered his own youth, when he felt the rules had been too strict, the devotions too long.

In our contemporary society, methods of presenting Scripture in family devotions may include using the family's creative gifts in acting, drawing, singing, and discussion. Whatever the format used, it seems right that the family's creative gifts be made an integral part of the experience.

Lawrence Richards, in *Religious Education*,[12] has some interesting observations on teaching the Word to children and youth that apply to any structured form of devotions in the home. He says he has come to understand when teaching children, he does not worry that he is giving them something that is beyond their ability to grasp. For even though they may not be able intellectually to understand forgiveness, he is helping them *experience* the reality of receiving forgiveness and extending it to others. In other words, regardless of age and stage of development, he is inviting the children to experience what scripture teaches. The challenge, Richards continues, is to link the Word with the *life* of the child so that he or she sees life from God's point of view. In this way, when temptation comes, anger surges, or alienation hurts, the experience triggers a biblical truth that will give the right perspective and help the child respond in a positive way.

Encouraging our children to use the privilege of free prayer is an important parental role. A friend says, "I remember my mother gathering us children around her so we could pray about problems that troubled her." Not only in confession of sin, not only in times of discouragement and fear, not only in intercession for others, Christian parents teach that prayer is "what you do." Parents teach that prayer also belongs to the exuberance of life, the "thanksgiving" days.

A life in which prayer is a big factor does not come easily. That is why we can help our children by encouraging the sharing of specific people and situations about which to pray. It is, for instance, indelibly imprinted on a child's memory if he or she hears a parent say his or her name in a prayer. And a parent gives a great gift to a child by encouraging what Frank Laubach[13] calls using "the chinks of time" for prayer—the in-between moments when one is walking down the corridor between classes at school, or waiting for a bus; in other words, in the normal flow of life as well as the structured times.

At a recent prayer breakfast for Search Institute, Barbara Varenhorst, author of *Real Friends* and *Peer Counselor Training*, shared the following story from memories of her own family life.

Each Saturday evening we had a family prayer service. Here is where I learned to pray for people who were in need, people who were in difficult situations. As a teenager I sometimes groaned when my mother prayed because her prayers were so long. My brother would try to get around this by saying quickly, "Barb, you pray tonight!" Nevertheless, my mother has been a model for me in her prayer life. She used prayer cards; she prepared prayer calendars for each day of the year, way up to the time of her death in her eighties. She did not just name the person or situation, she made one aware of the particular reason she brought their name before God.

Another specific way Mother's prayer life has been an example to me is that she encouraged my praying for a person who was making it difficult for me in some way. When I do that I have found that my attitude toward that person changes; I make constructive ways to settle our differences.

This is a heritage each parent can give his or her child.

Structured devotional times are planned by some families on celebration days. The Christmas festival, baptisms, birthdays, graduations, confirmations, anniversaries—all can attest to the fact that celebrations of life for the Christian family are inextricably linked with belief and faith.

In our family, we have a ritual each Christmas Eve. After reading of Scripture and singing—planned by different members of the family each year, and which all have a part in—the Christ Candle is lit. Then, one by one, beginning with the youngest, they go to the low table where the Christ Candle is surrounded by as many unlit candles as there are people present. Each in turn lights his or her candle from the Christ Candle and says, "I am lighting my candle because I want Jesus to light my way."

Structured devotional times during vacations capitalize on a period of the year when a family has time to be reflective. It is also a ritual in our family to set aside an hour at the end of a vacation to reflect on our experiences in relation to our faith. Equally meaningful statements come from the young child and the early adolescent as from the older teenager.

We have also observed the custom of having our own family service on Sunday mornings when on vacation. In this service, everyone has a chance to participate. The worship service has taken place in many settings. We've climbed on a Sunday morning to a point above a 12,000 foot pass, where we overlooked the formidable peaks of the Sawatch Range in the Colorado Rockies. As we sang the hymns, our voices were reminders of our smallness and God's greatness in this vast universe. We have sat on a rock in a cove of the Pacific Ocean beach as the tide came in. We have transformed an ordinary motel room into a place of worship. Each has served to provide a structured time of meaning and close fellowship.

Doing the Truth is Not an Adjunct to Shared Faith—It Is an Integral Part of It. Children in a family may learn their Bible stories very well, sing the songs of faith, feel a warmth in praying for each other, sense the kinship of believers in the family circle. But the totality of the shared faith experience is more than that. It is a combination of believing and doing. Sara Little, in *To Set One's Heart,* calls it "doing the truth."[14]

This third aspect of shared faith, namely, *doing the truth,* emerges in the study as a concept little thought about and seldom carried out. In spite of the fact that nearly 80 percent of the parents in the study indicate that religion is "the most important" or "one of the most important influences in my life," many do not see the connection between that and performing acts of love for others. Jesus' words, "I was hungry and you gave me food, . . . I was a stranger and you welcomed me, I was sick and you visited me," have seemingly not been attached in their minds to "religion."

We have given considerable emphasis throughout our book to the power of modeling. Yet, here we come to a situation in which the adolescents in the Adolescent-Parent study rank higher than the parents. Parents are considerably less likely than their children to believe that religious responsibility includes a horizontal dimension, that is, reaching out to help people in acts of love and mercy.

It is worthy of note that among adolescents in the Adolescent-Parent study who have a *concern for people,* one tends to find the following characteristics:

- Religious certainty
- The belief that religion is important
- Achievement motivation
- Positive self-image
- Concern about friendship
- Acceptance of traditional moral values.

Among fifth-graders and sixth-graders, there is a high correlation between a concern for people and a desire to work against poverty and for peace. As the march continues toward the ninth grade, however, this type of interest lessens. One possible reason for this is that parents tend to underestimate the interest and maturity of a child of eleven or twelve, and consequently do not give them opportunities to be part of a helping ministry. Wayne Rice, in *Junior High Ministry,* speaks of this age group as idealists even in the midst of their struggles, failures, and doubts.

For this reason it is important they be given many opportunities to serve and use the gifts God has given them. Their idealism, while it may be strong during the early adolescent years, will diminish over the years if not given expression, or it may be diverted into undesirable and destructive living. [Parents] should find as many ways as possible to channel the energies and enthusiasm of junior highers into service projects and other activities that allow them to give of themselves and to see the results of their efforts. They need to feel the significance and affirmation that such activities can give them. Junior highers desperately need to know that they are important and that God can use them right now.[15]

We remember a chance meeting with friends at an elegant restaurant some years ago. Their eighth-grade daughter had given them a bad time about their going out to eat that evening. She had learned at school about all the hunger in the world, and thought the money her parents were using to eat out should rather have been given to help someone in need. The mother especially was troubled and felt guilty. As we reflect on the incident now, we realize the greatest help we could have been to our friends and to ourselves would have been to discuss how we could involve our families in helping the hungry.

Such was the case with the father in the following true story,[16] told in the March 9, 1984 edition of the *Minneapolis Star and Tribune*. Frank Ferrell lived in a "well-off" suburb of Philadelphia. After seeing a TV presentation shortly after Christmas, he decided to take his eleven-year-old son, Trevor, into the downtown section so he could see firsthand how the street people live. They brought only a blanket and pillow to give to a needy person. The son was so profoundly moved and interested that he wanted his father to take him into town many nights a week with coats, jackets, soup, coffee, perhaps a bag of sandwiches. The boy "connects" his faith with these acts— he talks of being a minister when he grows up, and of establishing a permanent home for street people. But equally moving as the eleven-year-old's interest is the father's sensitivity in providing the opportunity for the boy to evidence his concern in concrete ways. By allowing children to give, we help them achieve a sense of worth.

To see one's acts of service as acts of faith are extremely helpful to an adolescent. Even in early childhood, families can have structured times of sharing faith which include Bible stories that tell of Jesus' caring for others. The next step is to relate the concept of caring to family life *in concrete ways*.

Edith Schaeffer, in an article entitled "What is a Family?" has this to say:

Human relationships on all levels are derived from essential childhood experiences. How to treat people is not a subject to be lectured about; it should be taught in real-life situations within a family.[17]

If parents were to take this statement seriously, they would be directly involved with their children in performing acts of service to others. One father and mother of young children tell of bringing the whole family along whenever they go to visit an elderly person who is homebound; the father, when he goes to remove snow from a neighbor's driveway, takes his five-year-old boy with him.

Bruce, a public school superintendent of a large suburban school district, now father of several adolescents himself, recalls a powerful modeling experience from his own youth.

July 17, 1961 was a hot humid Central Illinois day. My father, a farmer, was up at dawn to work in the fields. I was in graduate school and studied in the morning and helped him in the afternoon. About 5:30 P.M. Dad took me out to a neighbor's farm to get his truck. As I followed him back home, I saw him stop his truck on the edge of town where Harry Smith lived. Harry was considered a "bum," at least a person with no money, no friends, and no one who cared. As I drove by, Dad was walking around Harry's rundown house to see if he needed any food, transporation, or had needs of any kind. I remembered thinking as clearly as if it were yesterday, "Who besides Dad, tired as I know he is, would care so about another person's needs, especially when humanly speaking there is *nothing* in the world Harry could do in return."

Bruce goes on to say that his father had learned a lesson that the son is still learning—how to focus on another's needs, not his own. This example has caused the son to ask many times, "How can I show a person who is hurting that I care?" not "What's in it for me?" or "How will this affect me?"

Performing acts of love, if one sees the reason for doing so, can become a way of life. Alec Allen and Martin Mitchell, administrators of the Starr Commonwealth Schools in Albion, Michigan, had this demonstrated for them when they worked with troubled students who reside in family-style units. These students are part of an atmosphere designed to emphasize the positive values of caring, helping, trusting, and being responsible. These students learn that even if they are frightened in carrying out a project of helping someone else (e.g., a physically handicapped person), the thought that they can make that person's life better and safer by their act helps them overcome fear. Very positive things happen to these troubled students as a result of their service-learning. It would not be difficult to imagine some of the same benefits within a family unit under similar circumstances:

- They developed a bond of togetherness.
- They developed sensitivity to the needs and struggles of the mentally and physically handicapped, to the elderly, and to those facing death and disaster.
- They experienced the joy of helping.[18]

One young man said to a staff member, "Thank you for giving us the chance to know what it is like to help someone else." The staff noted that learning to help had long-lasting effects. A student named Eric left Starr to return to his home in Detroit, Michigan. Not long after, he went on his own to a section of Detroit where there were many nursing homes. He visited several of them to find out whether there were any residents who had no relatives or friends to visit them. Then he openly volunteered to visit those who needed a friend.

It is easy for a parent to fall into the trap of "arranging" for an act of kindness to be done by the adolescent for someone else. One mother, for instance, would offer her teenage daughter for babysitting, with no pay. Another mother and father invited a homeless family to stay with them for a period of time. As a result, night after night a resentful teenage daughter stood long hours in the kitchen washing dishes for the expanded family unit. In neither case was the adolescent girl part of the planning. Consequently, the acts of service were only negative experiences for her.

A positive experience occurred for Carolyn and Carl when, with the consent of their own two children, they welcomed four young brothers from Vietnam into their home. These four boys, all of whom were adolescents, had spent seventeen unbelievable days and nights on a boat, and two years in a camp in the Philippines. Now, a congregation witnesses the miracle of togetherness and love that has come as a result of the gift Carolyn and Carl gave of an open heart and open home.

To summarize, this chapter has drawn attention to a much neglected and overlooked source of strength—a shared faith. Though idealized as an important dimension of family life, the practice of sharing a religious faith in one's home is practiced by only a minority of church members.

The Adolescent-Parent study shows why this ancient tradition from Old Testament times ought to be revived. It can counteract a trend characteristic of early adolescents, namely, their growing disinterest in a religious faith. It provides also an opportunity for adolescents to deal with their growing issues of doubt and religious uncertainty. More importantly, a family-shared faith becomes a source of strength for young adolescents. It encourages them to avoid life-threatening behaviors and embrace those which are life-offering.

This chapter has drawn attention to the fact that sharing one's faith as a family can be done in a number of ways. It can be integrated into the everyday conversation of the family and made a part of the natural flow of the day. Or, matters of faith can be highlighted through structured times such as family devotions or festival times. Not least are the times when parents teach their children how to "do the truth" by participating with them in acts of service or kindness.

The data make it convincingly clear that families that take seriously the issue of sharing a religious faith give their children a remarkable legacy of strength.

7. Cry for Outside Help

> I can remember nights when we didn't sleep at all. I remember
> nights when I cried myself to sleep.
>
> —A DISTRAUGHT FATHER

Where does a parent turn for help?

That was the question asked by a perplexed father and mother
who had "given up" on their seventh-grade boy. Even the
public school would no longer keep him.

He had been changing in ways they thought were only the
marks of adolescence. But now he was becoming unmanagea-
ble: at times withdrawn, unwilling to study or go to school; at
times belligerent, hostile to authority, "spaced out,"
irresponsible.

Both mother and father—devout, caring and loving people—
spoke of sleepless nights filled with tears of despair, frustration, and guilt.

"Where have we failed?" they cried.

In desperation they consulted psychiatrists; this in turn led
to psychiatric clinics, a detoxification center, an adolescent
treatment center, a drug treatment center. There were parent
therapy sessions, too, and support group sessions. There was
Al-Anon. Things had gone out of control for mother and father
by this time. The distance between two people who cared
deeply for each other had been widening. Father blamed mother;
mother blamed father; and an older son and daughter blamed
them both.

Outside help? They grasped at it as they would a lifeline.

This chapter explores four important topics:

- Parents can't "go it alone"
- Four ingredients needed in outside help

- Six critical situations demanding outside help
- Clergy—a trusted resource

Parents Can't "Go It Alone"

If we stop to reflect, we will realize that as parents we have been the recipients of outside help all through our parenting lives. The nurse-friend who stayed with us around the clock during the birth of our first son . . . the neighbor who took a son to the hospital at midnight for emergency surgery when his father was out of town . . . the community uncles who coached the ball teams.

These are examples of the taken-for-granted forms of help we all accept, to one degree or the other, in the normal ebb and flow of family life.

Another stage of outside help is more consciously and deliberately accepted and used by parents. It is the information we gain about ways of parenting: the knowledge we seek in order to strengthen our children mentally, physically, and spiritually. Such meaningful help comes from books, workshops, seminars, and videotapes, which give both information and a conceptual framework for interpreting what we read and hear and see. This book itself is an example of outside help. Thirty-seven percent of mothers and 27 percent of fathers in the Adolescent-Parent study rate this kind of help highly.

In a recent session in which information on parenting was given, a couple who had celebrated their fiftieth wedding anniversary the year before were in attendance. Their reaction was very clear: "I wish we had had this kind of help fifty years ago, before we began raising our kids."

Today there is an added sense of urgency to know more about preventive measures in parenting. Our society has undergone a radical shift in values since 1965. This shift has been a movement to greater individualism, personal freedom, and tolerance for diversity, particularly personal indulgence. Some old moral absolutes have become quite relative. Many adolescents feel that "What I'd like to do is okay for me to do."

These changes have brought about serious problems for both youth and parents especially in six main areas: (1) drug use, (2) alcohol use, (3) sexual activity, (4) suicidal tendencies, (5) child abuse, and (6) other out-of-control behaviors.

We know that some of the desperate cries, such as we hear described in the illustration that begins this chapter, echo many times throughout the world of parenting. In this chapter, therefore, we are giving some pertinent information on each of these areas, some suggestions for home treatment that professionals who work in these fields have found helpful, and some guidelines for knowing when and where to go for professional help.

Especially in situations where it may mean loss of face, it is hard for a parent to ask for help outside the family. This is particularly true for parents whose own families never discussed family ills with "outsiders." Old timers know the hands-off expression, "Never soil your nest," meaning "Never say anything bad about your family." Asking for help is viewed by some parents as a sign of failure; this leaves them wide open to the assumption that every parent should be an expert in parenting.

Fortunately, parents today are coming to realize that it makes sense to draw on the skilled resources of an outsider when something needs to be fixed. If it's an income tax report, consult an accountant. If it's a car that gives trouble, see a mechanic. It's a sign of hope that of the 10,467 parents in the study, when asked whom they would turn to if facing a serious problem in their family, only 20 percent answered "nobody." The remainder said they would go to a relative, friend or neighbor, clergyman, medical doctor, school official, or community agency, depending on the problem involved. Figure 20 clearly identifies the clergy as a trusted source for parents. The relative few who would single out a school official (13 percent), medical doctor (17 percent), and community agencies (12 per-

Figure 20. Parents' Choices of Preferred Help on Problems*

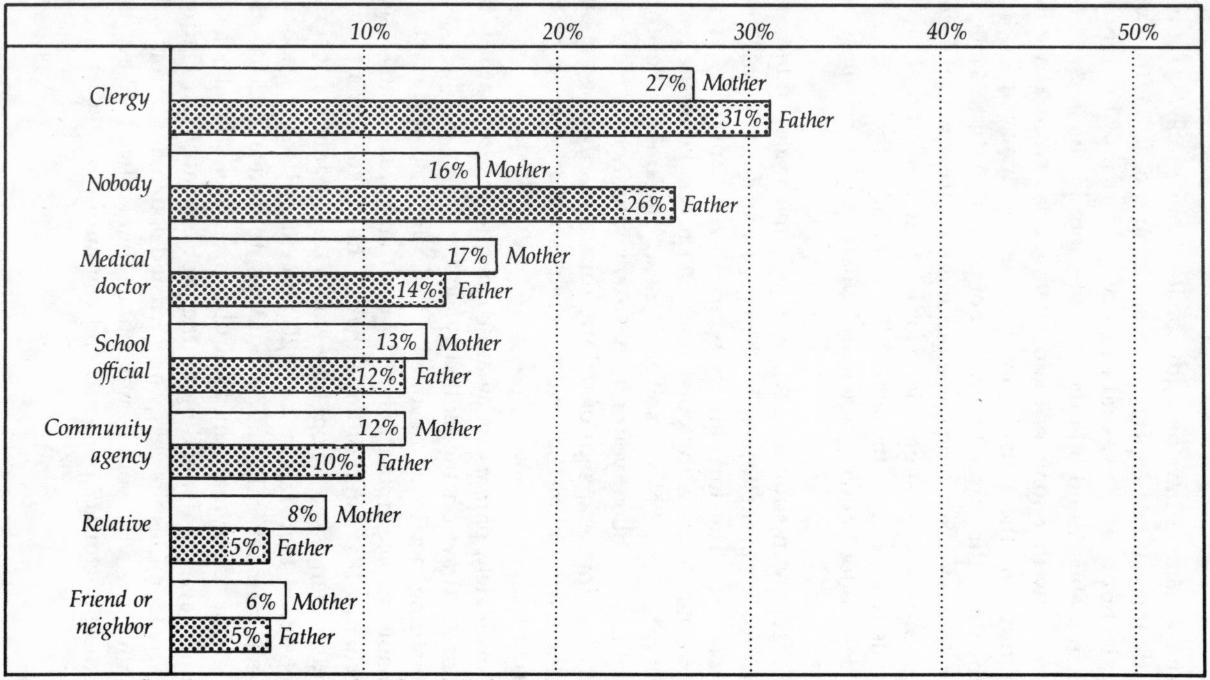

*Percentages reflect the parents responding *first choice* for each category.

cent) for preferred help may only indicate a general lack of awareness of the rich assortment of services available in a community. The pastor is often the facilitator for providing information on sources of help available; he or she can help parents gain access to remedial or educational programs.

The mother and father at the beginning of this chapter eventually availed themselves of many sources. For most communities, the principal ones are the pastor or a member of a church staff; a school counselor; a doctor or worker in the community health center; a family service agency (state or private); and youth-serving organizations such as the Y, Boy Scouts, Girl Scouts, Campfire, 4-H, Alcoholics Anonymous, Al-Anon, or Al-Ateen. Each one of these organizations has a surprising number of programs and services available to the family.

As parents our task is to discover the service that meets our special needs. It's like looking for a good restaurant. You don't give up on going to restaurants simply because one place served a bad meal. Likewise, parents should not let a poor experience with one person or program deter them from trying another source of help.

Four Ingredients Needed in Outside Help

No matter what problem parents are having with their adolescent, four elements are needed in the help they seek:

- Helpful support groups
- Esteem-building activities
- Positive belief system
- Own insight into self

These four comprise a model developed by Dr. Philip Shapiro.[1] Each ingredient supplies an important element in the healing process. We might mention, too, that in every instance of a parent-adolescent problem *both* parent and adolescent benefit from help.

Helpful Support Groups

Of importance to a person who needs help is to feel respected and esteemed, cared for and loved by a network of people. A social support group serves as a buffer during times of stress brought on by problems within the family; at the same time it provides healing and strength. This was the experience of the couple in the beginning illustration. The most powerful positive outcome for them came through a parent support group.

The universal experience is that just being in a support group has a calming effect. The invisible hand of human kinship is a therapeutic agent. A young woman who had been struggling with a number of decisions regarding personal morality remarked after a group meeting in which none of her own problems had been discussed, "I *needed* to come tonight. This was a great strength for me." In our nation today, there are over 40,000 national organizations of self-help groups. Their popularity proves that people who care about each other can be of mutual help without drawing on the expertise of professionals. The central ingredient of adult love and caring must figure prominently in any help a parent gives and receives.

Esteem-Building Activities

A second basic element is a set of activities that builds self-esteem. These may be work projects, recreational activities, training programs, or service projects. The essential element is that they breed a feeling of satisfaction and well being. They should give the troubled adolescent a feeling of accomplishment and significance.

A striking example of such activity is found in a service-learning program developed at the Starr Commonwealth Schools for troubled adolescents.[2] These youth are referred to the Starr presidential program because of police records, problems in family life, or poor school adjustment. At the same time as they are receiving treatment, they carry out more than one hundred community service projects during the year. They may serve as teacher aides, or work with retarded children, or chop firewood for the disabled, or visit shut-in senior citizens. The youth are shown how valuable their services are to the people involved; and intermingled with service they learn of constructive skills. The teachers of Starr Commonwealth report that these service-learning activities have helped their troubled adolescents develop increased responsibility and self-esteem. In fact, careful measures have shown striking gains in self-esteem over a three-year period. Parents themselves may find that becoming involved in a volunteer helping project at a time of family trouble is useful in giving them a sense of worth.

Positive Belief System

A third essential element in Shapiro's model is a positive belief system. It is a system of thought that one can use to gain a stable view of the world. It can also be used to determine one's identity, interpret life, maintain a sense of direction, and in general gain a sense of control and continuity in life.

There are two kinds of belief systems—one is pathological and the other healing. The pathological belief system consists of negative ideas, delusions, and incorrect conclusions held in a rigid and unyielding way. These can be held about oneself, one's family, one's world or one's God. We described in Chapter 6 how this is expressed theologically as a moralistic, guilt-producing concept of religion. The task for the help-giver is to correct the wrong ideas, change the person's beliefs about self, and help the person to accept the possibilities of desired changes.

One illustration of a pathological belief system is commonly seen in adolescents who are caught in a drug habit, alcoholism, sexual activity, or suicidal depression. They tend to believe they are no good, that they are not loved, and that the future holds no possibilities for them. They doggedly hold to the idea they are in control when using drugs, that peer acceptance will not allow the word "no," and that personal gratification ought not be delayed.

What is needed for these adolescents is the kind of help that brings another belief system into their consciousness—one that uses logic, includes adult love, and stresses a moral position. Often it is not the *words* of this new belief system, but *loving concern* that leads an adolescent to believe he or she is important, is loved, and has a future. Adolescents who are helped to internalize a moral code and identify with a personal God show the greatest likelihood of living responsibly and with the fewest hang-ups.

Ruth speaks of her experience with depression as a young woman: For me, as a Christian, the belief that I had infinite worth in the sight of God, that Christ had removed the element of judgment from me because of his redeeming love was life-giving for me. Scripture verses saying that nothing could separate me from the love of God, that the love of God had been poured into me, were powerful positive beliefs.

Own Insight into Self

A fourth component in the healing process of the troubled adolescent is self-knowledge or insight. For instance, if an adolescent is troubled with anxiety and depression after the death of a parent, he or she may be helped to see that these feelings are a natural aftermath of such a wrenching experience. The insight gained through such counseling can calm the fears the person may have had that he or she was "going mad." Even more, the adolescent may be helped to cope with depression by an awareness of the constant loving presence of God.

Perhaps the greatest, and the most necessary, help a professional counselor can give is in the area of a deeper level of insight, where the adolescent comes in touch with buried feelings long forgotten. This kind of insight can resolve, for instance, the strange dilemma of holding the belief "I love my mother," while at the same time battling strange feelings of rage and hatred for her.

This last component of the healing process, namely insight into oneself, may not come without pain. It is at this point that the supportive group, the esteem-building activities, the strength found in positive beliefs about oneself and one's God, are the bulwarks that bring the adolescent—and perhaps the parent, too—into a state of mental and spiritual health.

As parents look at these four basic ingredients needed in an outside help program, they might ask themselves the following questions about a program they are considering or are already participating in: Are supportive groups developed or used? Does the program make use of activities to develop a sense of self-worth? Are positive beliefs about oneself and God being established? Does the program encourage and lead one into greater self-knowledge and insight?

Notice that these four ingredients, placed in a certain order, spell the word HOPE.

Helpful Support Groups
Own Insight into Self
Positive Beliefs
Esteem-Building Activities

Six Critical Situations That Demand Outside Help

Drug Use

During the 1960s and 1970s, use of all illicit drugs increased twenty-fold, and the use of marijuana increased thirty-fold. What began with university students in the early 1960s spread downward in age through high school to junior high school. When Dr. Armand Nicholi finished his scholarly review of the research on drug abuse, he chose as subtitle for his article the words "A Modern Epidemic": "Use of psychoactive drugs has spread with explosive force into an epidemic of extraordinary scope, involving all regions of the country, all socio-economic classes and all age groups."[3]

Marijuana, the most used drug (next to alcohol) and the most defended in the past, has effects that justify serious national concern. It affects intellectual functioning, memory, sensory and perceptual functions, and reaction time—a fact that contributes to the high incidence of automobile accidents among young people. Its use can precipitate psychotic reactions, impair lung function, and affect the immune and reproductive systems. Those using the drug regularly have less motivation, perform more poorly in school, have fewer religious convictions, and are more involved in antisocial and delinquent behaviors such as stealing, vandalism, and truancy. Though the use of marijuana declined in the 1980s, in 1990 it still ranks second to alcohol as church youth's preferred drug. Among the juniors and seniors involved in the *Effective Christian Education* study, one in five (19%) had used marijuana at least once in the past year, in contrast to 3 percent who had used cocaine.[4] The same contrast typifies youth in the 1990 study, *The Troubled Journey*.

Behaviorial scientists have consistently found that student drug use is largely a social activity. But Richard and Shirley Jessor at the University of Colorado have found that while experimentation with drugs is related mainly to environmental opportunities, deep involvement correlates best with low self-esteem.[5] Young people with poor self-images are drawn to drug use whenever it occurs, finding in it a common bond with other troubled youngsters, which may lead them into increasing isolation from non-drug-involved peers and activities. These processes generally start between the sixth and twelfth grades. It is usually most helpful to give students who have a firm sense of self-respect accurate information about the physical and psychological risks of drug use.

What Parents Can Do. The biggest hurdle for parents is to accept the fact that the child they love and care for has become involved in the use of drugs. Denial is an almost universal defense mechanism. It is a common experience to hear a mother say of her teenager, "I can't understand it; Judy used to get such good grades in school. This year she just doesn't seem to care." Or, "I don't like the friends Judy is running around

with. They're all different from the ones she had last year."
Yet this mother is quick to add, "But I know she isn't using
drugs. She'd never do that," even though the evidence clearly
points in that direction.

Parents are advised to bring their teen to a drug counselor
if they suspect a problem. It is much better to be told by a
counselor that you don't need professional help than to let a
problem become more severe, and consequently more difficult
to deal with. There should be no hesitation about seeking a
therapist immediately if your teenager is using amphetamines,
barbiturates, Angel Dust, cocaine, acid or heroin. Use of marijuana shows up in behavior such as lack of responsibility,
grades dropping off in school, or a change in circle of friends.

Because the family is involved, drug education must begin
with parents. In the booklet *Never Too Early, Never Too Late,*
members of a Chemical Awareness Committee in a Minnesota
school district have given a number of guidelines for parents
who suspect more than incidental use of drugs by their teenager. This set of guidelines is furnished by Hazelden, a drug
treatment center.

- *Confront the issue.* Be open and honest about your feelings.
- *Don't minimize and deny.* Parents want to believe otherwise.
- *Set standards.* Parents need to say "no" clearly and firmly.
- *Don't ask why.* Work with what's happened rather than
  trying to determine why it happened.
- *Ask for help.* There are many confidential sources available
  to parents. Call your school, police, or community agency
  for information on sources of help.[6]

Although only one person in the family may be singled out
as an abuser, the whole family needs to be involved in treatment. A family is an interactive system in which all members
affect and are affected by each other. A strong tendency found
in addictive families is a dependent need for each other. As a
result, addicts tend to continue living with their families of

origin well into their late twenties. They use drugs to escape their family without actually leaving them.

Because families are such an interactive system, the treatment of choice for drug addiction is family therapy. It provides a way by which parents can be helped to relinquish control and the addicted member helped to establish a sense of autonomy. The goal of family therapy is to enlist the family as an ally in the treatment process. Through participation, the family learns how to survive without needing a chemically abusive member.[7]

Alcohol Abuse

Because of groups like Mothers Against Drunk Driving (MADD) and Students Against Drunk Driving (SADD), the public is now aware of the immense social and personal costs of alcohol abuse. As many as 15 million Americans have severe drinking problems. Three million are under 18 years of age. For motorists sixteen to twenty-four years old, alcohol-related car crashes are the leading cause of death. In a given two-week period, almost half the high school seniors of our country have been drunk. Search Institute confirms this finding in their 1990 study, *The Troubled Journey,* in which a total of 55 percent of the seniors reported having consumed, during the last two weeks, five or more drinks in a row.[8] This, for most, is equivalent to becoming intoxicated. This high incidence of drinking to excess is 9 percent higher than the percentage found for high school seniors in a 1983 Minnesota study. The implications of widespread teenage drinking are disturbing and the stories being told are tragic.

In the spring of 1983 one of the authors met with the Division Director of Mental Health and Developmental Disabilities in the state of Alaska, Dr. Philip Shapiro. Though experienced in the ghettos of Harlem, he was profoundly shaken by a three-day visit to an Alaskan village. There he found three hundred natives in despair over the fact that in a period of six months, thirteen young people had died of suicides or alcohol-related deaths.

Though alcohol-related problems have always been with us, at no time in our history has the issue been one of such magnitude and pervasiveness. What has been suspected for centuries is now a known fact. Fetal alcohol syndrome, a severe and irreversible syndrome of birth defects, is one of the three most common causes of mental retardation.[9] A fair approximation of the situation in 1983 is that alcohol abuse is linked to half of all automobile accidents, half of all homicides, 25 percent of all suicides, and about 40 percent of all problems brought to family court. It is estimated that the cost of alcoholism to society is about $10,000 per problem drinker.[10] Yet in today's society, athletic heroes do TV commercials telling youth it's OK to drink; their peers are insisting that a weekend party is dull without plenty of beer or hard liquor.

Virginia Edwards writes:

Ours is a drinking society. All the great rites of human passage are celebrated with booze. Births and christenings, birthdays, graduations, weddings, promotions, divorces, deaths and funerals all include drinking of alcohol. Holidays and festivals revolve around the fellowship of the glass. We even have parties where alcohol is the guest of honor—the cocktail party, the beer bash, and the wine-tasting party make no secret of that. We drink to promote a deal and to close one, when the team wins and when it loses, when we're relaxed with friends and tense with strangers. It's when kids get the impression that we *need* to do this that they're off to a bad start.[11]

That message is being heard. In 1990, 51 percent of the eighth graders in *The Troubled Journey* study had already tried drinking, and 22 percent had in the last two weeks imbibed 5 drinks or more in a row.[12]

The cry for outside help arises out of real, not imagined concerns. It relates to a threat that is being intensified by profiteering adults anxious to sell their products. The tragedies connected with their use is sufficient to justify an all-out war. That is how parents, banding together under the title MADD, view their activity. Incensed over deaths of their children caused by drunk drivers, they are working for more stringent legislation to restrict drivers that drink.

"No alcohol for kids under drinking age except in the case of religious or ceremonial use," decrees Dr. Neil Hartman of Cornell University Medical College, New York City. A specialist in substance abuse, he sees so many adolescents in deep difficulty with drugs that he has no patience with parents who play alcoholic games with their children. "Offering kids drinks or sips of drinks shows psychopathology in the parent that is akin to child abuse," he says firmly. "Total abstinence for those under 18 is a good goal. These are the years when personality is forming, and alcohol interferes with sound social and sexual development."[13]

Parents need to realize that teenage drinking often is a reflection of adult drinking habits. Families that have a tradition of heavy drinking can expect the same from their adolescents. Teen drinkers follow a well-developed set of folk rules in their drinking that corresponds to the unspoken social rules followed by adults.[14]

What Parents Can Do. The best way to help adolescents avoid alcohol abuse is to provide them with accurate, undistorted information about alcohol, a good example, and firm moral guidelines.

Parents ask, "How can I tell if my child is drinking?" Experts and cynical young drinkers have a counter-question. "How can you *not* know?" Parents' resolute blindness to their youngsters' drinking is one of the most familiar aspects of the alcohol problem.

A wild tirade, specialists warn us, isn't the answer. Postpone the talk until the youngster is sober and you are calm and in control. Encourage the youngster to analyze the reasons for his or her loss of control.

If the incident is repeated, it's time to show a different kind of concern. Drunkenness is not natural or understandable; it is a state of illness. In the opinion of Ellen Morehouse, a third incident should bring punishment, swift and immediate (denial of going to an event the youth may have looked forward to). More than three incidents calls for strong intervention, she feels. "Point out that 'we're a family with a problem. You are drinking, and I am not getting through to you.' Don't wait until the situation is out of control and the kid's marks are dropping, he's cutting classes, getting into fights, seeing a whole new world of friends." Typically, parents do wait until the problem is entrenched.[15]

As parents, it is vital that we allow youngsters to suffer the consequences of their irresponsible drinking. Experts agree on this. Don't try to "squash" traffic tickets, or hush up incidents involving the police "for the family's sake." For the kid's sake, let him or her deal with the results of his or her own actions.

Adolescents, not the parents, should make amends for property damage, either by making repairs or earning the money to pay for them. They should deal directly with the people they have injured when out of control. *"Don't do anything to make it easier for the kid to drink,"* urges Betty Karnay, specialist in adolescent treatment at Princeton House, Princeton, NJ.

When reasoning, firmness, and strong limits—and even a couple of bad experiences—haven't stopped out-of-bounds drinking, parents must seek outside help.[16]

Where to Get Help. Following is a list of people to contact. Assume that a person and a program can be found that fits your situation.

School. Contact the chemical health coordinator or community educations director of your local school district. If these do not exist in your school system, consult the school counselor or principal.

Work. Contact your employer as to whether or not your place of work has an employee assistance program.

County. Contact your county social service and health service agencies. They can refer you to public and private treatment centers, counseling and mental health clinics, detoxification centers, half-way houses, and services for assisting in chemical dependency.

Community Groups. Check into groups such as Alcoholics Anonymous, Al-Anon, and other support programs. Your local service organizations such as Jaycees, Kiwanis,

Knights of Columbus, and local youth serving organizations such as 4-H, Campfire, or Boy Scouts may have programs.

Church Pastor. Remember, this person can be of great assistance in helping you find the right help for a specific adolescent or family situation.

Sexual Activity

A third critical issue is the growing incidence of premarital sexual activity among adolescents. Some profound changes in our society have occurred with respect to sexual freedom. Between the years 1967 and 1974 nonmarital intercourse rates increased about 300 percent for white females and 50 percent for white males.[17] Since then there has been a continuing rise in nonmarital intercourse, with adolescents becoming involved at younger and younger ages. Illegitimate births are seen as undermining black families. The percentage of fatherless black families tripled between the 1960s and the early 1980s.[18]

The Adolescent-Parent study found that one in five ninth-graders have had sexual intercourse at least once. This was true for 28 percent of the boys. These statistics and trends alert us to the fact that a sexual revolution did indeed occur in the late 1960s and early 1970s.

There are factors in the life of an adolescent that break down good resolves, making sexual activity not only desired, but inevitable. Chilman, in her comprehensive review of studies on adolescent sexual activity, singles out the following major factors associated with nonmarital intercourse: "low level of religiousness, permissive societal norms, racism and poverty, peer-group pressure, friends who are sexually active, low educational goals and poor education achievement, deviant attitudes, strained parent-child relationships and minimal parent-child communication, age (older than sixteen) and early puberty.[19]

Most parents are not willing to acquiesce to the idea that no matter what we say, "teenagers are going to be sexually active." This assumption, they maintain, sells young people short; for it is telling them in effect that they're incapable of self-discipline and they're not intelligent enough to make choices for purposes greater than self-gratification. A society that settles for teenage sexual activity also fools adolescents into thinking they're mature enough at age thirteen and fifteen and seventeen to handle all the emotional, psychological, social, and moral consequences of premature sex.

What Parents Can Do. Teenagers want to hear a clear statement, with reasons, as to why they should resist teenage pressures to become involved in sexual intimacies. Parents should realize that the most important sex organ is still the one found between an adolescent's ears: the brain. Because feelings begin in the brain, young people can back away from being overwhelmed by pressures and peer society norms.

Most parents want help in learning how to talk with their adolescent about sex. Some are uncomfortable when talking about the facts and feelings of sexuality, especially when it involves their children. Others, though willing to be their children's teachers, have questions concerning *when* children should be taught about sexuality, *what* details should be conveyed, and *how* the information should be presented. Few parents want to admit their ignorance about human sexuality, or to sound ignorant on the subject before their children. As a result many parents feel the need for support and training in communicating a stance on sexuality that commends both responsibility and restraint.

Where to Get Help. An aid to parents is available in video-assisted programs of instruction in sexuality, for use in schools and churches. Each course, introduced first to parents, is a values-based program designed to develop a sense of reverence for this aspect of God's creation and to promote responsible restraint. The tapes are used to introduce difficult-to-discuss topics, thus making it easier for parents to talk about matters of sexuality with their adolescents. Dr. John Forliti, has developed the training program for use in public schools and Roman Catholic congregations and schools. The need for such instruction can be seen in the growing percentage of youth making themselves vulnerable to unhappy futures, such as sexually transmitted diseases like AIDS. In the 1990 *Troubled Journey* study, 52 percent of the seniors surveyed admitted to having had sexual intercourse four or more times.[20]

Parents should take advantage of resources such as these:

Denominational Social Services. Major denominations have excellent staff and programs in major cities and towns to serve parents and teenage parents. Your pastor can help you locate the appropriate one.

Family Services. A network of 250 Family Service agencies provides confidential services at fees based on ability to pay. Information about them may be obtained by contacting United Way in your community. Crisis intervention services for families and individuals are available immediately for those whose situation is seen as critical.

Adolescent Suicide

Throughout history, suicide has been considered a mysterious act and, in most societies, a taboo subject. But the sharp rise in adolescent suicides since the 1960s has made it a subject of great concern. For adolescents aged 15–19, there has been a 312% increase in suicides between the years 1957 and 1987, almost twice the increase reported for 21 to 24 year olds.

In an article in *Lutheran Standard,* Steve Swanson cites illustrations from both a wealthy suburb and a rural area.

Psychiatrists in Chicago speak of the suburban North Shore—one of the richest areas of the country—as the Suicide Belt. With median family incomes exceeding $60,000, teenagers there grow up in beautiful neighborhoods, go to the best schools, and materially at least, have much of what they want. Porsches and Jaguars pepper the high school parking lots. Yet 28 North Shore teenages in a 17-month period killed themselves—18 by gunshot, eight by hanging, and two by lying down in front of trains.

This isn't only a problem that threatens suburban youth. A small town in North Dakota has been touched by this tragedy, too. In a seven-month period, three young people killed themselves. A fourth youth, age 16, died of a handgun wound that authorities believe was self-inflicted. As that rural community struggled with the issue of suicide and its prevention, a hospital chaplain cautioned the people against 'denial of reality' and a feeling of not wanting to talk about this concern for fear of disrupting the community.[21]

Causes. The causes of suicide are complex and numerous. Each case involves a different combination of reasons, but they are mainly cradled in the difficulties of adolescent years. Here, in order of importance, are the major causes that current research has isolated.[22]

Depression. This is the most common emotion felt by a suicidal person, but it is not always easy to detect.

Loss of parent. Loss by death, divorce, separation, or extended absence can have a devastating impact on an adolescent. While loss of parent usually does not precipitate a suicide, it can influence adolescents in that direction.

Alienation from family. When family ties are close, suicide rates are low; and where the ties are not close, the rates are high. Alienation comes when communication breaks down because of family conflict or stress on high achievement in school, sports, or social relationships.

Other contributing causes. For some adolescents, death holds a mystical or magical attraction. For others, strong sex drives create inordinate feelings of guilt. Still others are frightened by world events and have lost all hope of a significant future. Some have an overwhelming need for perfection. Change of address, breakup with a girlfriend or boyfriend, and inability to cope with a situation are all additional factors.

Warning Signs. Given these major causes, what does a parent watch for as warning signs?

Verbal signs include frequent comments similar to these: Direct comments like "I wish I were dead"; or indirect statements such as "No one around here needs me" or "Why is there so much unhappiness in life?"

Behavioral signs include extreme mood shifts, sudden changes in behavior, an unsuccessful suicide attempt.

Depression is the most prevalent indicator of suicide. Symptoms of depression are varied: fatigue; loss of appetite and energy; marked drop in quality of schoolwork and grades; withdrawal from friends; spending much time alone; difficulty in sleeping or, in some cases, excessive sleeping; preoccupation with talk about suicide; giving away prized possessions; feelings of guilt; helplessness or anxiety; expressions of hopelessness; despair; low self-esteem; delinquent behavior; sexual promiscuity; drug and alcohol abuse.

What Parents Can Do. When parents become aware of warning signals, the best preventive measure is to listen. Give the adolescent a chance to talk freely. (See Chapter Three on Listening for Understanding.) For a suicidal person, friendship from a peer can avert disaster. It may be difficult for a peer to give this friendship to a person at school who may be labeled "weird" or "unfriendly" because he or she feels alienated; but we as parents need to encourage this kind of friendship on the part of our adolescents. *At the same time,* parents should contact a person skilled in suicide prevention and bring the adolescent into a counseling relationship.

Where to Get Help. Over two hundred suicide prevention centers across the country are staffed around the clock, seven days a week. These centers operate an immediate crisis service by telephone. The purpose of this service is to provide emotional support to the caller and direct the person to sources of help. A list of suicide prevention centers may be obtained by writing to the American Association of Suicidology, 2459 South Ash, Denver, Colorado 80222.[23] Also useful is a 1991 publication of the American Psychological Association entitled *Adolescent Suicide* by Alan Berman and David A. Jobes.[24]

A remarkable story of hope was found in a *New York Times* article about William Fox, an officer in the New York police department.[25] He was successful in persuading Michael Buchanan, a young teenager, not to jump from a Bowery flophouse roof, while people in the street below shouted, "Jump, jump!" The appeal that got through to the boy, whose mother died when he was two and whose father was an abusive alcoholic, was this: the bachelor police officer promised to take him to his home, where he could have a room and could go to school. When he was finally rescued, the boy, with tears in his eyes, asked William Fox, "Did you really mean what you said?"

William Fox did. Michael became his foster son and was soon attending school and drawing respectable grades. Finding an adult who would love and care for him changed his life dramatically. A book written about the two, entitled *To Make a Difference,* became a two-hour CBS television movie.

Child Abuse

The September 1983 issue of *Time* magazine[26] focused on the serious national problem of interrelated private acts of violence known as child abuse, wife-beating, and rape. Of these, child abuse was singled out as being the "ultimate betrayal."

Murray Straus, in a research study of 1,146 families,[27] found that approximately fourteen of every one hundred children between the ages of three and seventeen experience an average of 10.5 episodes of violence per year. These alarming data are supported by statements of many reporting agencies that the instance of child abuse and neglect are not less than the above, but more. The growing awareness of the magnitude of child abuse has led to it also being labelled a "disease epidemic."

The Search Institute study showed that one in five of the 8,165 young adolescents worry that "someone might force me to do sexual things I don't want to do." One in four worry ("somewhat," "quite a bit," or "very much") that "one of my parents will hit me so hard that I will be badly hurt." A physical abuse index in this study showed that parents who are abusive also tend to be coercive, nagging, drinkers who use autocratic methods of control and excessive punishment. Their children tend to rebel against their authority, acquiesce to peer pressure, and be fearful of sexual aggression. Each of the characteristics identified above with parents and youth correlates well with the index of physical abuse.

Mary Otto, in her review of the research on child abuse notes that abusive parents are not necessarily poor or uneducated, though poverty and lack of knowledge do cause additional stress in families, and therefore account for a somewhat higher rate of abuse in poor families.[28] Child abuse exists at all social levels.

Typically, abusive parents are lonely, isolated, insecure individuals who have very little psychological or social support from their families. They lack meaningful communication with their partners, parents, or siblings. They usually have few friends or valued social outlets. They have an overwhelming sense of isolation. Though they may wish to stop their abusive behavior, they lack the skill and support to make and maintain constructive changes.

Physical abuse carries the most visible scars and draws the most outraged reactions. But it is second to emotional and sexual abuse in its devastating effects on a child.

Linda Halliday, in her autobiographical account entitled *Silent Scream*,[29] tells of her emotional reactions to sexual intercourse with her father from the ages seven to sixteen. The experience drove her to attempt suicide several times; she turned to alcohol and prostitution, and then to date only men who were physically and sexually abusive to her.

Like a poisonous plant sending out its spores, family violence reproduces itself. Most rapists were preyed upon sexually as children; most violent criminals were raised in violent homes. Battered children grow up disposed to batter their own offspring.

What Parents Can Do. These frightening, ugly details are difficult for parents to read or agree to. To have sexual abuse come from a stranger is easier to accept and warn against than when it occurs within one's own walls or within one's larger family or neighborhood unit.

Those who work in the area of child abuse suggest that parents begin to use preventive measures when a child is very young. For example, a parent could teach a child at an early age how to distinguish between a "good touch" and a "bad touch," between feeling "safe" in the company of an adult or feeling "threatened." A number of good books and teaching aids available through libraries and child protection agencies give helpful suggestions in carrying out preventive measures. It is important that children are taught to *tell someone* if they feel confused or bad about something someone has done to them. A parent might explain that sometimes people we love have problems and don't act appropriately. When we feel confused or unhappy about what someone says or does to us, we should talk about it.

Children find it extremely difficult to "tell" if the offender is a parent, because often the only form of security, livelihood, and love they know is tied up in their home. In some cases, an offending parent has put an unbelievably heavy burden on a child by saying, "If you tell, I will be put in jail, and it will be your fault." For that reason alone, it is rare for a child to lie about sexual abuse.

A parent should believe the child, even if it hurts. A child may throw out hints, hoping the parent will guess; perhaps an ambiguous statement elaborated on from time to time. This is called testing the parent to see if the subject could be open for discussion. At this point *reflective listening*, as discussed in Chapter 3 could be put to good use.

A child protection assessment worker in Dakota County, Minnesota, gave this advice at a workshop:

If you as a neighbor, friend or relative, hear a child, however obliquely, refer to his or her parent as abusive, listen carefully to what is being said and attempt to ask sensitive questions that will not frighten the child. It's important not to promise the child that action will be taken to stop the abuse. Broken promises are something that the child may be all too accustomed to. Rather, you might reassure the child that you care, that you will continue to listen and would like to ask the help of someone accustomed to handling such problems. While only certain professional people are mandated to report suspected child abuse and neglect to the authorities, any person may do so.[30]

Symptoms of sexual abuse are also indicators of other problems. It is the combination of these symptoms that may lead to an unfolding of the problem and subsequent help. Symptoms that have sexual overtones are the ones most likely to mean the presence of sexual rather than physical abuse.

Possible Symptoms of Child Abuse. The following are symptoms you should watch for in your child.

1. Dramatic changes in school behavior; withdrawal, depression, acting-out
2. Moderate to severe depression or anxiety
3. Fear of going home
4. Fear of being touched
5. Excessive fear of adults (male or female)
6. Running away from home, especially when it is habitual
7. Chemical/alcohol abuse or dependency
8. General self-destructive tendencies: includes chemical addiction, involvement in delinquency, suicide attempts or ideation, involvement in destructive relationships, adolescent prostitution
9. Poor peer relationships
10. Extremely low self-esteem
11. Inability to trust others, fear of the outside world
12. Poor personal-care skills
13. Regressive behavior such as bedwetting, thumb-sucking
14. Frequent nightmares
15. Unusual disgust for sexual matters
16. Sexual acting out, lack of appropriate boundaries
17. Unexpected sexual utterances (sounds or words, phrases) especially from small children

18. A facade of maturity; especially in teenage girls who are given adult roles to fill in the family
19. Excessive masturbation in children
20. Regression in developmental milestones
21. Clinging behavior
22. Open sexual behavior after age five to seven
23. Physical symptoms:

- burns, cuts, bruises appearing regularly or on unlikely parts of the body
- fractures that don't fit the description of the incident
- unexplained abdominal pain
- body mutilation (self-inflicted tatoos, cigarette burns, cuts)
- venereal disease—oral, genital, anal
- adolescent pregnancy
- pain on defecation
- vaginal discharge in girls, urethral discharge in boys
- oral fissures or other unexplained lesions, gagging response or chronic sore throat
- sudden weight gain or loss—especially in teenage girls

Where to Get Help. Most communities have child protection agencies, community mental health centers, or police departments who can give needed help. If the abuse is occurring within your own immediate or extended family, you should confront the offender as well as seek outside help. Breaking the secrecy that surrounds the abuse is therapeutic. However, it is also important to recognize that the root causes underlying abusive behavior and its scarring effects usually need professional intervention in order to break the cycle of abuse.

Because abusive parents are consistently described as being isolated, lonely, and lacking in support, the help given them must be a response to these conditions. Although individual counseling offers help in some areas of the parents' life, it does not provide the ongoing support system that alleviates the isolation and loneliness.

A more helpful approach is *group counseling.* Membership in such a group provides parents with an immediate support system and a chance to reduce their overwhelming sense of isolation. In such support groups, parents are encouraged to contact each other between meetings and they are required to call a specified person when they are about to abuse a child. This making of a definite break between feeling and behavior reduces impulsiveness. The result is a sharp reduction in physical and verbal abuse, even after only two sessions of the group.

Group counseling provides a mechanism by which abusive parents can be distracted from themselves and their problems, learn to share with others like themselves, and come to understand how best to handle their anger. A peer group is effective because it not only supports parents but also demands the reduction of violent behavior.[31] A national association of support groups called Parents Anonymous (patterned after Alcoholics Anonymous) is an available help.

Parents should know that if sexual abuse has been a factor in the home, in most cases it indicates the lack of a loving, supportive discipline system. The children have heard many angry and abusive words; physical violence has often been used to control them. Parents in such homes may be suffering from depression, anxiety, and problems of controlling their anger. They need outside help in learning how to redirect anger and aggression into appropriate behaviors. They need help in learning to show love to their children. There may be marital conflicts in such a home, alcohol abuse, difficulties in relationships with friends and relatives. Sometimes there is the stress of poverty, poor housing, employment problems, and single parenthood. These factors are often a part of the vicious cycle of perpetuating family violence.

Other Out-of-Control Behaviors

More than half the cries for help that reach child-guidance clinics are for problems such as defiance, fighting, lack of cooperation, and lying. Characteristic signs of such out-of-control children include:

- Physical: hitting, vandalizing, stealing
- Verbal: sarcasm, yelling, defiance
- Attitudinal: negative, defeatist
- Emotion: lack of affection, manipulative use of affection

Children who *frequently* display these behaviors are often called "incorrigible," or "social deviants," or "problem children."

Every parent has seen these behaviors in a child. What distinguishes out-of-control adolescents is the frequency with which these behaviors occur. In the study of 8,165 adolescents, 5 percent admitted to having damaged property or stolen from a store six times or more during the year. Twice that many (11 percent) acknowledged having hit or beaten another six times or more. One out of four (23 percent) admitted to having lied to one of their parents six times or more during the last twelve months. These are the kind of adolescents who are candidates for the label "out-of-control" youth. Accompanying their norm-breaking or aggressive tendencies are often the following characteristics:

- They associate with peers who are prone to the same kind of deviance
- They are frequently in conflict with their parents
- They are uninterested in school
- They are conscious of their peers violating school regulations
- They report high exposure to movies and TV

Significantly, a 1982 report by the National Institute of Mental Health, which reviewed a decade of studies on the effects of television on children especially scored television violence. It found almost all studies that were reviewed support the conclusion that watching violence on television leads to aggressive behavior by children.[32] Television viewing has the effect of heightening a state of general arousal—it can produce an emotional response.

Need for Discipline. Studies have found that out-of-control children *do* respond to discipline that is consistent, nonabusive, and rationale-giving. The solution seems to lie in helping parents to become more effective disciplinarians.

For discipline to be effective, it should be used consistently and then, after the punishment is over, the parents should emphasize the child's positive responses.

What Parents Can Do. An excellent program for parents with out-of-control difficult children has been developed by Fleischman, Horne and Arthur, the authors of *Troubled Families.*[33] With minimal additional training, professionals with a B.A. or M.A. degree can make this training available in a religious institution, community mental health center, child guidance clinic, protective service agency, juvenile department, or school. The program, aimed to assist parents with behavior problems, emphasizes home-based rather than institutional treatment. It can be conducted in groups and used in a variety of social service, congregational or psychological settings. It uses a step-by-step sequence for building skills and transferring responsibility for change from teacher to parent. When tested over a two-decade period, it has proved highly effective in altering the behavior of out-of-control children. In bringing children to accept adult authority and control, it accomplishes what they want of their parents—clearly identified limits. (Described below are six disciplinary procedures recommended to parents in the program, with special emphasis on handling difficult children. Though uniquely effective with out-of-control children, parents should note that these procedures can be preventive medicine, applying equally well to children not out-of-control.)

Time-Out is a type of punishment often used when a child hasn't done what he or she has been told to do and has a defiant attitude. It also is an effective discipline when there is fighting going on between siblings. In time out, a parent isolates the child for a few minutes after each instance of misbehavior. Children who are six years or older who refuse to go to time-out should be warned once. If they still refuse to go, then a privilege is taken away.

Grandma's Law is a good procedure for enforcing various rules, routines and responsibilities set up in a household. It is essentially non-confrontative, deriving its name from the legendary grandmother who told her grandchild, "First you eat your vegetables, then you can have some pie." What the rule really means is that parents insist children do whatever has been asked of them or expected of them. Then and only then can the children do what they want. If a child ignores the parent and follows his or her own wishes, a time-out results. Sometimes the alternative is to lose a privilege or be assigned extra work.

Natural and Logical Consequences. "Natural consequences" could be defined as what would normally happen with no adult intervention, and "logical consequences" as letting the punishment fit the crime. These are ways to deal with children who act irresponsibly or like to let the parent do the work for them. Using such consequences means that the parents will no longer cover for the children or protect them from the negative consequences of their behavior. For example, a parent refuses to join in a frantic hunt for schoolbooks that have been misplaced by a child, or a mother won't rewarm a meal for a child who comes home late, or a parent requiring a child who damages something to pay for its repair. Following natural and logical consequences works best when these irresponsible actions have become patterns of behavior, and thus the parents have opportunity to decide well beforehand how they will carry out the intended consequences.

Some parents, especially those who tend to be overly protective, may find it hard to let their children suffer the consequences of their actions. The parents feel guilty about not coming to help their child. For this reason, parents who seriously consider using natural or logical consequences as a form of discipline should discuss between themselves the pros and cons of this technique; they may develop a list of positive self-statements to assist them in following through without feelings of guilt.

Withholding Attention as a procedure works best with small children who pester their parents for attention, sometimes by whining, pouting, or pretending to cry. If parents consistently ignore these behaviors, they usually will see a dramatic decrease in their occurrence. The child will increasingly use attention-getters when the parents first withhold attention, thinking it will eventually "work." Parents need to withstand this initial *increase* in annoying behavior by recognizing that their child is testing this new discipline. Should the child's testing get too severe, the parent should be prepared to use time-out as a punishment.

Taking Away Privileges. When a child tests the parents' use of time-out, Grandma's Law, or withholding attention, then parents can remove privileges. Loss of privilege is also a good consequence when a family member fails to attempt or complete part of an agreement. Used this way, it's the most appropriate consequence for older children ("If you're home late, you can't watch TV after dinner.") Allowing no desserts or snacks, denying use of the telephone, not letting the child ride his or her bike, not letting an adolescent play the stereo are all common procedures of removing privileges. A discipline especially difficult for a gregarious teenager is to take away the privilege of having friends over. When using this method, most parents make the mistake of taking away too many privileges and for too long a period of time (grounding a child for a week). It's generally more effective to withdraw fewer privileges for a shorter time—for example, losing an hour of TV time or having to go to bed 30 minutes early. Except in special circumstances the privilege should be lost for no longer than twenty-four hours after the misbehavior has occurred. This is important for parents to remember.

Assigning Extra Work. With more serious offenses, including lying, stealing, damaging property, and causing problems at school, this procedure is effective. The amount of extra work should be based on the seriousness of the behavior. For example, white lies might earn fifteen minutes of work; stealing one to two hours. To discourage the child from simply dawdling over the assigned chore, the parents should identify the amount of work they expect to be done (for example, if one is asked to clean the bathroom, it means scouring the sink, tub, and toilet, and mopping the floor). Observing this simple procedure can save angry words between adolescent and parent. Parents should also expect the work to be done well and, until the job is finished to the parents' satisfaction, they should deny the child access to any privileges.[34]

These methods, developed over time and proven to be effective, illustrate parenting that is firm, rational, and caring. They establish the parent as being the person in charge.

This matter of learning to accept the authority of one's parents is a basic ingredient in the life of an adolescent. When it is missing, one tends to find adolescents who rebel against any requirement that crosses their wishes. As a result of such rebellion the adolescent often becomes involved in at least one of the six critical behaviors described here. Living without clear limits and a firm authority figure is similar to living under an extremely permissive type of parental control. The effect is to encourage a self-centered and self-indulgent child. By way of contrast, a discipline that teaches young people to accept and respect authority prepares them for the realities of life, the authority of the workplace, of marriage, of living under governments, of a moral universe.

Clergy—A Trusted Resource

Over the years, people have sought out clergy as their first choice when turning to someone for help during a personal crisis. Clergy are a trusted resource. When faced with seven problem situations involving their adolescent, and asked who would be their first choice for help or advice, parents in the

Adolescent-Parent study gave clergy the highest average response. Of course, the answers vary according to the problem. For instance, if the problem is depression, a medical doctor is the first choice. The same is true when one's child is asking difficult-to-answer questions about sex (though other professions may be more knowledgeable regarding the emotional, moral, or spiritual aspects of sex). The one problem most parents assume they can best handle alone is the problem of their child hanging around with kids the parents don't like. Here they are inclined to ask nobody. Aside from these exceptions, the pastor is clearly seen as a preferred source of help.

When these parents rated the help given by their clergyperson, nearly half used the rating of "very" or "quite" helpful. Clearly, a significant proportion of today's population is pleased with the help made available to them through their pastor. One can conclude that many members of the clergy, through their programs of clinical pastoral education, have become skilled in providing support and making referrals to agencies that specialize in certain services.

As one distraught woman explained, "I was so depressed over the problem with my fourteen-year-old son that I couldn't think of a single place to go for help—except to my pastor. I called him and found the help I needed. He was great!"

It is an expectation of church members that they can look to clergy and the community of faith for help in times of stress. In fact, it is associated with their concept of effective ministry. Documentation for this comes from the Readiness for Ministry study conducted by Search Institute and referred to in Chapter 3. When laity and clergy who were randomly selected from forty-seven denominations indicated which characteristics they regarded as most important in a clergyperson, their second-from-the-top choice was "ministry to people in times of stress." People in congregations want their pastor to be especially sensitive to people who are going through times of physical, emotional, or spiritual stress. They also want members of the congregation to be equipped to serve as a caring community and as a friendship/support network. Though this form of ministry in most congregations is an emerging service, whatever exists is appreciated. The evaluations given by parents in the Adolescent-Parent study show that programs, books, and printed materials made available by congregations have been helpful.

Help is wanted as much by parents of girls as of boys. Though fathers lag behind mothers in saying they are much interested in the kinds of help identified in the survey, more that half say they are "very" or "quite" interested in key services related to the five cries of parents. A responsibility of parents is to make this desire known to the clergy and local church councils. Here are the average percentages of 10,457 parents declaring much interest in:

70%   How to help a child develop healthy concepts of right and wrong (Moral Purpose)

68%   How to help a child grow in religious faith (Shared Faith)

66%   More about drugs (Outside Help)

62%   How to communicate better with one's children (Close Family)

47%   Effective discipline (Close Family)

44%   More about sex education (Understanding One's Adolescent)

42%   How to participate in a parent support group (Understanding Oneself)

It is interesting to note that the percentages of parents wanting this help show little variation from fifth to ninth grades. The kinds of help parents want do not vary by the age of their child. More importantly, they relate directly to the issues discussed in this book.

As parents we should note that adolescents are also open to help from their congregation—help related to the very areas of special concern to parents. Half of the adolescents declare much interest in programs that coincide with their parents' top interests, namely, help related to

- figuring out what it means to be a Christian
- learning about what is right and wong

Two out of five adolescents want to "learn how to talk better with adults."

Of special note is the adolescent's interest in topics related to their own greatest concerns:

- learning how to make friends and be a friend (61 percent)
- finding out what is special about me (51 percent)

Without question, clergy and their congregations form a unique and trusted resource for the parent.

A Final Word

This book has identified five desires or cries of parents. Each cry represents a parent reaching out in order to become a better parent. Each cry focuses on a basic issue in the home. And each cry points to a highly significant and available source of strength.

This book addresses parents in a day of epidemics—a time when social diseases are laying claim to an increasing number of adolescents. Rather than try protecting our child from the toxins of life, we should concentrate on strengthening the inner life of the child.

In summary, these sources of strength include the following:

A close but open family life

This is possible when parents

- demonstrate love and affection in their relationships with each other
- communicate well with their adolescent and each other

- teach responsible living through consistent authoritative-type discipline
- show affection, respect, and trust to their child

Moral beliefs and purpose

Encouraged by parents who

- seek to live within the universe of traditional moral beliefs
- have a life orientation that is not moralistic or self-centered
- model a life that carries a sense of responsibility for others' needs
- help adolescents internalize moral beliefs by using rational explanations of what is right or wrong

A personal, liberating faith

Encouraged by parents who themselves

- have a faith that is liberating rather than moralistic and restrictive
- share their experiences of faith with members of the family
- discuss the Scriptures and pray together with their adolescent
- model "doing the truth" by helping where there is need

The support of caring people

Made possible by a parent's willingness to

- accept the help of others
- become part of a support network of caring adults
- seek help when one's adolescent is involved in:
  — drug abuse
  — alcohol abuse
  — sexual activity
  — suicidal tendencies
  — child abuse
  — other out-of-control behaviors

- learn methods of discipline that are consistent, firm, and fair.

These are the sources of strength adolescents need.

These are the elements of parenting which we as authors have experienced as sources of strength. We share them not only because they have enriched and enlivened our family but also because research based on thousands of families identifies them as sources of strength. Parents who feel beleaguered while battling against seemingly impossible odds, should take heart. The sources of strength presented here are live options for every parent. They can be answers to the cries which occasioned the writing of this book. Undergirding these answers is the caring God who revealed himself in Jesus Christ. We have found that "He is faithful who promised." He does intervene in the life of a family, to reshape values, attitudes, and relationships, and to unite members in a bond of love.

Notes

Chapter 1. A Time of Danger and Opportunity

1. Search Institute is a nonprofit organization, founded in 1958. Its mission is scientific, pioneering research on issues faced by service and religious organizations and action based on the research to effect desired changes. During its 25-year history, SI has been located in Minneapolis, Minnesota. Its mission is carried out through three separate activities: searching for answers to questions involving human need by means of research; sharing this information with those who need it; and consulting with organizations to help them act on the information they receive.

   Though Search Institute has specialized in the study of young people, it also conducts major studies of institutions and people who serve youth. Hence, the institution has conducted such studies as a Readiness for Ministry project involving the seminaries and congregations of 47 denominations, a study of Catholic high schools in the '80s, and a study of the religious beliefs and values of the 96th Congress.

2. David Olson and Hamilton McCubbin, *Families: What Makes Them Work* (Beverly Hills: Sage Publications, 1983), 219, 221.

3. Kay Pasley and Viktor Gecas, "Stresses and Satisfactions of the Parental Role," *Personnel and Guidance Journal* 62 (1984): 400–404.

4. Gail Sheehy, "The Crisis Couples Face at 40," *McCalls* 103, (May 1976): 107.

5. Eda LeShan, *The Wonderful Crisis of Middle Age* (New York: McKay Publishing Company, 1973).

6. Documentations for all references to the Adolescent-Parent study can be found in the following publication, available through Search Institute: Peter L. Benson, et al., *Young Adolescents and Their Parents* (Minneapolis: Search Institute, 1984).

7. Hamilton McCubbin, Anne Thompson and Phyllis Pirner, *Family Rituals, Typologies, and Family Strengths* (University of Wisconsin: Family Stress, Coping and Health Project, 1986), 54, 98–99.

8. Peter Benson and Carolyn Eklin, *Effective Christian Education: A National Study of Protestant Congregations* (Minneapolis: Search Institute, 1990).

9. Peter Benson, *The Troubled Journey: A National Portrait of American Youth* (Minneapolis: Search Institute, 1990).

10. Letty Cottin Pogrebin, *Family Politics* (New York: McGraw Hill, 1983), 25–26.

Chapter 2. The Cry for Understanding Yourself as a Parent

1. Kurt Andersen, "Private Violence," *Time* 122 (September 5, 1983): 19.

2. Robert Reineke, *Report to the National Board of American Lutheran Church Women on a Study of Attitudes of Women* (Minneapolis: Search Institute, 1981).

3. David Mace, "Love, Anger and Intimacy," *Light* (April-May 1980): 2.
4. Haim G. Ginott, *Between Parent & Teenager* (New York: Avon Books, 1969), 96.
5. *Ibid.*, 97.
6. *Ibid.*, 100.
7. Joan Bordow, *The Ultimate Loss* (New York: Beaufort Books, 1982), 52.
8. *Ibid.*, 81.
9. *Ibid.*, 89.
10. This analysis is based on data from the Adolescent-Parent sample. The 482 single parents who participated in the study were compared to the entire population of mothers from intact families.
11. John Guidibaldi, "The Impact of Parental Divorce on Children: Report of the National NASP Study," 1983.
12. *Ibid.*
13. *Ibid.*
14. David Jolliff, "The Effects of Parental Remarriage on the Development of the Young Child," *Early Child Development and Care* 13 (1984): 321–334.
15. C. Gilbert Wrenn, *The World of the Contemporary Counselor* (Boston: Houghton-Mifflin, 1973).

Chapter 3. Cry for Understanding Your Adolescent

1. We have adopted these goals from a conceptual scheme developed by John Hill in *Understanding Early Adolescence: A Framework* (Carrboro: Center for Early Adolescence, University of North Carolina, 1980).
2. Larry K. Brendtro and Arlin E. Ness, *Re-Educating Troubled Youth* (New York: Aldine Publishing Company, 1983), 15.
3. *Ibid.*
4. Peter Benson, *The Troubled Journey: A National Portrait of American Youth* (Minneapolis: Search Institute, 1990), 71.
5. Amy Harris, "He Doesn't Believe in Handicaps," *Faith at Work* 91 (October 1978): 51.
6. Barbara Varenhorst, *Real Friends: Becoming the Friend You'd Like to Have* (San Francisco: Harper & Row, 1984).
7. Grace W. Weinstein, "Should Teenagers Work?" *McCall's* (June 1983): 54.
8. *Ibid.*
9. *Ibid.*
10. Fritz Ridenour, *What Teenagers Wish Their Parents Knew About Kids* (Waco: Word Books, 1982), 40.
11. Roland Larson and Doris Larson, *I Need to Have You Know Me* (Minneapolis: Winston Press, 1979), 35–36.
12. Francis Iaani, *Eight-Year Study of Teenagers* (New York: National Institute of Education, 1984).
13. Varenhorst, *Real Friends,* 58.

Chapter 4. Cry for a Close Family

1. Letty Cottin Pogrebin, *Family Politics* (New York: McGraw Hill, 1983), 25.
2. David H. Olson and Hamilton McCubbin, *Families: What Makes Them Work* (Beverly Hills: Sage Publications, 1983), 231.

3. Merton P. Strommen, *Five Cries of Youth* (San Francisco: Harper & Row, 1974), 47.
4. Augustus Y. Napier and Carl A. Whitaker, *The Family Crucible* (New York: Bantam Books, 1978).
5. Strommen, *Five Cries of Youth*, 42.
6. Ellen Goodman, "For Tsongas and His Family, a Discovery of the Preciousness of Time," *Boston Globe* (17 January 1984).
7. Charlie Shedd, *Promises to Peter* (Waco: Word Books, 1970), 116.
8. Diana Baumrind, "Authoritarian vs. Authoritative Parental Control," *Adolescence* 3, no. 11 (Fall 1968): 261.
9. Merton P. Strommen, Milo L. Brekke et. al. *A Study of Generations* (Minneapolis: Augsburg Publishing, 1972), 390.
10. Strommen, *Five Cries of Youth*.
11. Baumrind, "Authoritarian vs. Authoritative Parental Control," 256.
12. *Ibid.*, 269.
13. Dave Capuzzi and Lindy Low Le Coq, "Social and Personal Determinants of Adolescent Use and Abuse of Alcohol and Marijuana," *Personnel and Guidance Journal* 62, no. 4 (December 1983): 200.
14. Francis J. Ianni, "Community, Adults Mold Teens, Study Says," *Minneapolis Tribune*, March 25, 1984.
15. David Augsberger, *When Caring Is Not Enough* (Scottsdale, AZ: Herald Press, 1983), 270.
16. Fritz Ridenour, *What Teenagers Wish Their Parents Knew About Kids* (Waco: Word Books, 1982), 83.
17. Jane Norman and Myron Harris, *The Private Life of the American Teenager* (New York: Rawson, Wade Publishers, 1981), 37.
18. Dolores Curran, *Traits of a Healthy Family* (Minneapolis: Winston Press, 1983), 99.
19. *Ibid.*, 103.
20. Lee J. Stromberg, "Meet Hamilton McCubbin: He's Testing Family Tension," *Correspondent* (Winter 1983): 9.
21. George Armelagos, "Culturally Speaking: A Tasty Tale," *Weight Watchers Magazine* 14 (February 1981): 9.
22. Olson and McCubbin, *Families*, 150.
23. Dolores Curran, *Traits*, 102.
24. Larry K. Brendto and Arlin E. Ness, *Re-Educating Troubled Youth* (New York: Aldine Publishing, 1983), 63.
25. *Ibid.*, 63.

Chapter 5. Cry for Moral Behavior

1. C. S. Lewis, *Abolition of Man* (New York: Macmillan Press, 1946), 95–121.
2. Lawrence Kohlberg, "Continuities and Discontinuities in Childhood and Adult Moral Development Revisited," in *Collected Papers on Moral Development and Moral Education*, Harvard University, 1973.
3. Carol Gilligan, *In a Different Voice* (Cambridge: Harvard University Press 1982), 19–20.
4. Lawrence Kohlberg, *The Philosophy of Moral Development*, Vol. 1 (San Francisco: Harper & Row, 1981), 345.

5. Merton P. Strommen, *Five Cries of Youth* (San Francisco: Harper & Row, 1974), 106.
6. David Rosenthal, "The Year in the Movies," in *Rolling Stone Yearbook* 25 (1983), 25–26.
7. Harry Haun, "Loss of Innocence Remains a Commercial Constant," *Denver Post*, August 12, 1983.
8. Peter Benson and Carolyn Eklin, *Effective Christian Education: A National Study of Protestant Congregations* (Minneapolis: Search Institute, 1990), 33–35.
9. William Raspberry, "It's Time for Black Adults to Make Teenage Virtue a Necessity," *Washington Post*, August 7, 1984.
10. Dolores Curran, *Traits of a Healthy Family* (Minneapolis: Winston Press, 1983), 185.
11. Peter Benson, *The Troubled Journey: A National Portrait of American Youth* (Minneapolis: Search Institute, 1990), 71.
12. Peter L. Benson, Dorothy L. Williams, *Religion on Capitol Hill: Myths and Realities* (New York: Harper & Row, 1983), 154–163.
13. Strommen, *A Study of Generations*, 243.
14. Robert Coles, Lecture at Westminster Presbyterian Church, Minneapolis, Minnesota, February 1984.
15. *Ibid.*
16. Alan Keith-Lucas, *The Client's Religion and Your Own Beliefs in the Helping Process.* Group Child Care Consultant Services, Aug. 1983, 12–15.
17. Peter L. Benson, *et al. Young Adolescents and Their Parents* (Minneapolis: Search Institute, 1984), 288.
18. *Ibid.*

Chapter 6. Cry for a Shared Faith

1. Dolores Curran, *Traits of a Healthy Family* (Minneapolis: Winston Press, 1983), 216.
2. Lee J. Stromberg, "Meet Hamilton McCubbin," *Correspondent* 81, no. 520 (Winter 1983).
3. Carl Reuss, *Profiles of Lutherans* (Minneapolis: Augsburg Publishing House, 1983).
4. Princeton Religious Research Center. *Religion in America*, 1981.
5. Benson, Peter L. and Eklin, Carolyn H. *Effective Christian Education: A National Study of Protestant Congregations* (Minneapolis: Search Insitute, 1990), 25, 46.
6. Peter Benson, *et. al., Young Adolescents and Their Parents* (Minneapolis: Search Institute, 1984).
7. Sara Little, *To Set One's Heart* (Atlanta: John Knox Press, 1983), 13, 15, 17.
8. Paul Johnson, *Psychology of Religion* (Nashville: Abingdon Press, 1959).
9. Peter Benson and Carolyn Elkin, *Effective Christian Education: A National Study of Protestant Congregations* (Minneapolis: Search Institute, 1990), 26.
10. David Augsburger, *When Caring Is Not Enough* (Scottsdale: Herald Press, 1983), 110–111.
11. Karen Mains, *Open Heart, Open Home* (Elgin: David C. Cook, 1975), 16.
12. Lawrence Richards, "The Teacher as Interpreter of the Bible," *Religious Education* 77, no. 5 (September-October 1982): 515, 516.

13. Frank Laubach, *Prayer* (New Jersey: Fleming H. Revell, 1946), 56.
14. Little, *To Set One's Heart*, 76.
15. Wayne Rice, *Junior High Ministry* (Grand Rapids: Zondervan, 1978), 112–113.
16. Associated Press, "Boy, 11, Who Aids Street People is Honored by Philadelphia Council," Minneapolis *Star and Tribune*, March 9, 1984.
17. Edith Schaeffer, "What is a Family?" *Living and Growing Together* (Waco: Word Books, 1976), 22.
18. Alec J. Allen and Martin L. Mitchell, "Helping the Community: An Untapped Resource for Troubled Children," *The Pointer* (Fall 1982): 1–4.

Chapter 7. Cry for Outside Help

1. Philip Shapiro, "A Treatment and Management Model," *Coping Magazine* (April 1983): 11–20, 27–30.
2. Larry K. Brendtro and Abraham W. Nicolaou. "Hooked on Helping," *Synergist* 10 (Winter 1982): 38–41.
3. Armand Nicholi, "The Nontherapeutic Use of Psychotic Drugs," *New England Journal of Medicine* 308: 925–933.
4. Peter Benson, *The Troubled Journey: A National Portrait of American Youth* (Minneapolis: Search Institute, 1990), 87.
5. Jeffrey Mervis, "Adolescent Behavior: What We Think We Know," *APA Monitor* (April 1984): 24, 25.
6. Hazelden Foundation, *Never Too Early, Never Too Late* (Hazelden Foundation, 1983), 14–15.
7. Russell A. Haber, "The Family Dance Around Drug Abuse," *Personnel and Guidance Journal* (March 1983): 428–430.
8. Peter Benson, *The Troubled Journey: A National Portrait of American Youth* (Minneapolis: Search Institute, 1990), 87.
9. Sheila Blume, "Prevention of the Fetal Alcohol Syndrome," Paper prepared for National Council on Alcoholism (June 1983).
10. *New York Times.* "High Cost of Alcoholism Staggers Economy," November 1983.
11. Virginia Edwards, "Teenage Drinking," *Scouting* (October 1982): 76.
12. Peter Benson, *The Troubled Journey: A National Portrait of American Youth*. (Minneapolis: Search Institute, 1990), 87.
13. Edwards, "Teenage Drinking," 78.
14. Dave Capuzzi and Lindy Low Le Coq, "Social and Personal Determinants of Adolescent Use and Abuse of Alcoholism and Marijuana," *Personnel and Guidance Journal* (December 1983): 199–205.
15. Edwards, "Teenage Drinking," 80.
16. *Ibid.*
17. Catherine S. Chilman, "Coital Behaviors of Adolescents in the United States: A Summary of Research and Implications for Further Studies." Prepared for meeting of APA, 1983. Unpublished paper.
18. Ray Marshall, "Youth Employment/Unemployment/Underemployment: A Continuing Dilemma," (St. Paul: Center for Youth Development and Research, 1983).
19. Chilman, "Coital Behaviors."

20. The course, *Values and Choices,* written by Dr. John Forliti, is available from Search Institute, 122 West Franklin, Minneapolis, Minnesota, 55404.
21. Steve Swanson, "Teen Suicide," *Lutheran Standard* 24, no. 3 (February 3, 1984): 11.
22. Lynda Y. Ray and Norbert Johnson, "Adolescent Suicide," *Personnel and Guidance Journal* (November 1983): 132–133.
23. F. Wenz, "Self-injury behavior, economic status and the family anomie syndrome among adolescents," *Adolescence* 14, 387–397.
24. Berman, Alan L. and Jobes, David A. *Adolescent Suicide: Assessment and Intervention.* American Psychological Association: Washington, D.C., 1991.
25. Judy Klemesrud, "Officer Saved A Life and Gained A Son," *New York Times.* Appeared in *Minneapolis Tribune* April 4, 1982.
26. Ed Magnuson, "Child Abuse: The Ultimate Betrayal," *Time* (September 5, 1983): 20–22.
27. Murray Straus, Family Patterns and Child Abuse in Nationally Representative American Sample, *Child Abuse and Neglect* U.S. Government Publication Report printed in 3, 1979.
28. Mary Otto "Child Abuse: Group Treatment for Parents," *Personnel and Guidance Journal* (February 1984): 336.
29. As quoted in Magnuson, "Child Abuse," 21.
30. Judy Strommen, Child Protection, Dakota County, Minnesota. Talk given to Parish Education Directors, Minneapolis, Minnesota, November, 1982.
31. Otto, "Child Abuse," 338.
32. Eli Rubenstein, "Television and Behavior," *American Psychologist,* July 1983, 820–821.
33. Matthew J. Fleischman, Arthur M. Horne, and Judy L. Arthur, *Troubled Families* (Champaign: Research Press, 1983).
34. Quoted from disciplinary procedures presented in *Troubled Families* by Fleischman, Horne and Arthur, 1983.

Bibliography

Allen, Alec J. and Martin L. Mitchell. "Helping the Community: an Untapped Resource for Troubled Children." *The Pointer* (Fall 1982): 1–4

Andersen, Kurt. "Private Violence," *Time* 122 (September 5, 1983): 18–19.

Armelagos, George. "Culturally Speaking: A Tasty Tale." *Weight Watchers Magazine* 14 (February 1981): 9.

Associated Press. "Boy, 11, Who Aids Street People is Honored by Philadelphia Council" *Minneapolis Star and Tribune,* March 9, 1983.

Augsburger, David. *When Caring is Not Enough.* Scottsdale: Herald Press, 1983.

Ausubel, David P., Raymond Montemayor, and Pergrouhi Svajian. *Theory and Problems of Adolescent Development.* 2d ed. New York: Grune and Stratton, 1977.

Bachman, Jerald G., Johnson, Lloyd D., O'Malley, Patrick M. *Monitoring the Future* (1988). Institute for Social Research; University of Michigan, 1991.

Baruch, Dorothy W. *How to Live With Your Teenager.* New York: McGraw Hill, 1953.

Baumrind, Diana, "Authoritarian vs. Authoritative Parental Control." *Adolescence* 3 (Fall 1968): 255–270.

Benson, Peter L. Highlights from 1983 Colorado Survey on Drug Use and Drug-Related Attitudes, a project conducted by Search Institute, Minneapolis, in cooperation with KRHA-TV, Colorado Department of Education. Research Report.

Benson, Peter L. Report on Drug Use and Drug-Related Attitudes. State of Minnesota. Minneapolis: Search Institute, October 25, 1983.

Benson, Peter L. *The Troubled Journey: A National Portrait of American Youth.* Search Institute: Minneapolis, 1990.

Benson, Peter L. and Carolyn H. Eklin, *Effective Christian Education: A National Study of Protestant Congregations.* Search Institute: Minneapolis, 1990.

Benson, Peter L. and Dorothy L. Williams. *Religion on Capitol Hill: Myths and Realities.* New York: Harper & Row, 1982.

Benson, Peter L. et al. Young Adolescents and their Parents. Minneapolis: Search Institute, 1984.

Berman, Alan L. and Jobes, David A. *Adolescent Suicide: Assessment and Intervention.* American Psychological Association: Washington, D.C., 1991.

Better Homes and Gardens, eds. *What's Happening to American Families?* Los Angeles: Meredith Corp., 1983.

Blume, Sheila. "Prevention of Fetal Alcohol Syndrome." Paper prepared for National Council on Alcoholism, Washington, D.C., June 1983.

Bordow, Joan. *The Ultimate Loss.* New York: Beaufort Books, 1982.

Brekke, Milo L., Merton P. Strommen, and Dorothy L. Williams. *Ten Faces of Ministry.* Minneapolis: Augsburg Publishing, 1979.

Brendtro, Larry K. and Arlin Ness. *Re-Educating Troubled Youth.* New York: Aldine Publishing, 1983.

Brendtro, Larry K., and Abraham W. Nicolaou. "Hooked on Helping." *Synergist* 10 (Winter 1982): 38–41.

Briggs, Dorothy Corkille. *Your Child's Self-Esteem.* New York: Doubleday, 1975.

Buntman, Peter H. and Eleanor M. Saris. *How to Live With Your Teenager.* Pasadena, California: Birch Tree Press, 1977.

Bustonoby, Andre. *The Readymade Family.* Grand Rapids: Zondervan Publishing, 1982.

Capuzzi, Dave and Lindy Low Le Cog. "Social and Personal Determinants of Adolescent Use and Abuse of Alcohol and Marijuana." *Personnel and Guidance Journal* 62 (December 1983): 199–205.

Chilman, Catherine. "Coital Behaviors of Adolescents in the U.S." Paper prepared for meeting of The American Psychological Association, 1983.

Chilman, Catherine. "Parent Satisfactions, Concerns, and Goals for Their Children." *Family Relations* 29 (1980): 339–345.

Collins, Gary. *How to Be a People Helper.* Ventura: Vision House, 1976.

Collins, Gary, ed. *Living and Growing Together.* Waco: Word Books, 1976.

Cunningham, Susan. "Abused Children are More Likely to Become Teenaged Criminals." *APA Monitor* (December 1983): 26, 27.

Curran, Dolores. *Traits of a Healthy Family.* Minneapolis: Winston Press, 1983. Discussing in particular fifteen traits commonly found in healthy families by those who work with them, this book is easy to read and full of practical insights and personal illustrations on what constitutes a strong, vibrant family.

Dickson, Charles. "Parents Can Help Their Children Learn to Live." *Lutheran Standard* 22 (February 1983): 10.

Dobson, James C. *Hide or Seek.* Old Tappan, New Jersey: Fleming H. Revell Company, 1974.

Dobson, James C. *Straight Talk to Men and Their Wives.* Waco: Word Books, 1980.

Donnelly, Katharine Fair. *Recovering from the Loss of a Child.* New York: Macmillan, 1982.

Duvall, Evelyn Millis. *Faith in Families.* New York: Rand McNally, 1970.

Edwards, Virginia. "Teenage Drinking." *Scouting* (October 1982), 76–80.

Elliott, David J. and Norbert Johnson. "Fetal Alcohol Syndrome: Implications and Counseling Considerations." *Personnel and Guidance Journal* 62 (October 1983): 67–69.

Fleichman, Matthew J., Arthur M. Horne, and Judy L. Arthur, *Troubled Families.* Champaign: Research Press, 1983.

Gallup, George, and David Poling. *The Search for America's Faith.* Nashville: Abingdon Press, 1980.

Gelles, Richard J. *Family Violence.* Vol. 4, Sage Library of Social Research. Beverly Hills: Sage Publications, 1979.

Gilligan, Carol. *In a Different Voice.* Cambridge: Harvard University Press, 1982.

Ginott, Haim G. *Between Parent & Child.* New York: Avon Books, 1969.

Ginott, Haim G. *Between Parent & Teenager.* New York: Avon Books, 1969.

Gordon, Sol and Judith Gordon. *Raising a Child Conservatively in a Sexually Permissive World.* New York: Simon and Schuster, 1983.

Greenfield, Guy. *The Wounded Parent.* Grand Rapids: Baker House, 1982. Written by parents whose children (teenagers and young adults) have rejected the spiritual values of their parents, this book attempts to provide both immediate and long-range help. It suggests ways in which parents might rebuild the channels of communication with their children and construct new relationships with them after the "break" has occurred.

Guidibaldi, John. "The Impact of Parental Divorce on Children." Report of the National Association of School Psychologists (NASP) Study. 1983.

Haber, Russell H. "The Family Dance Around Drug Abuse." *Personnel and Guidance Journal* (March 1983): 428–430.

Harris, Amy. "He Doesn't Believe in Handicaps." *Faith at Work* 91 (October 1978): 20–21, 51, 63.

Hazelden Foundation. *Never Too Early, Never Too Late.* Center City, MN: Hazelden Educational Materials, 1983.

Hill, John P. *Understanding Early Adolescence: A Framework.* Carrboro: Center for Early Adolescence, University of North Carolina, 1980.

Johnson, Paul. *Psychology of Religion.* Nashville: Abingdon Press, 1959.

Jolliff, David. "The Effects of Parental Remarriage on the Development of the Young Child." *Early Child Development and Care,* 13 (1984): 321–334.

Kamerman, Sheila B., and Cheryl D. Hayes, eds. *Families that Work: Children in a Changing World.* Washington, D.C.: National Academy Press, 1982.

Keith-Lucas, Alan. *The Client's Religion and Your Own Beliefs in the Helping Process: A Guide for Believers and Non-Believers.* Group Child Care Consultant Services, Chapel Hill, NC, 1983.

Kohlberg, Lawrence. "Continuities and Discontinuities in Childhood and Adult Moral Development Revisited." *Collected Papers on Moral Development and Moral Education.* Cambridge: Harvard University Press, 1973.

Kohlberg, Lawrence. *The Philosophy of Moral Development. Vol. 1 of Essays on Moral Development.* San Francisco: Harper & Row, 1981.

Lagaard, Nora G. and Robert P. Goelz. "The Best-Kept Secret: Sexual Abuse." *Campfire Leadership Magazine* (October–December 1983): 5–7.

Landorf, Joyce. *Change Points.* Old Tappan, New Jersey: Fleming H. Revell Company, 1981.

Larson, Roland and Doris Larson. *I Need to Have You Know Me.* Minneapolis: Winston Press, 1979. This workbook, containing fifty exercises for couples to complete together and alone, is an excellent book for couples who want to take a look at their relationship. Participants evaluate their communication skills, measure their relational progress, and discover ways to enrich their marriage relationship.

Laubach, Frank C. *Prayer.* New York: Fleming H. Revell Company, 1946.

Lerman, Saf. *Parent Awareness.* Minneapolis: Winston Press, 1980.

LeShan, Eda. *The Wonderful Crisis of Middle Age.* New York: McKay Publishing Company, 1973.

Lewis, C. S. *The Abolition of Man.* New York: Macmillan, 1947.

Lewis, Margie M. *The Hurting Parent.* Grand Rapids: Zondervan Publishing House, 1980.

Lipuma, Ann. "The Forgotten Child." *McCall's* 110 (September 1983): 32.

Little, Sara. *To Set One's Heart.* Atlanta: John Knox Press, 1983.

Mace, David. "Love, Anger and Intimacy." *Light* (April–May 1980): 2.

McCubbin, Hamilton I., Anne I. Thompson, and Phyllis A. Perner, *Family Rituals, Typologies, and Family Strengths.* Family Stress, Coping and Health Project: Univ. of Wisconsin, 1986.

McGinnis, Alan Loy. *Friendship Factor.* Minneapolis: Augsburg Publishing, 1970.

Magnuson, Ed. "Child Abuse: The Ultimate Betrayal." *Time,* 122 (September 5, 1983): 20–22.

Mains, Karen Burton. *Open Heart, Open Home.* Waco: Word Books, 1971.

Markun, Patricia Maloney. *Parenting.* Washington, D.C.: Association for Childhood Education, 1973.

Marshall, Ray. "Youth Employment/Unemployment/Underemployment: A Continuing Dilemma." St. Paul: Center for Youth Development and Research, 1983.

Mervis, Jeffrey. "Adolescent Behavior: What We Think We Know." *APA Monitor* (April 1984): 24, 25.

Naisbitt, John. *Megatrends: Ten New Directions Transforming Our Lives.* New York: Warner Books, 1982.

Napier, Augustus Y., and Carl A. Whitaker. *The Family Crucible.* New York: Bantam Books, 1978. In a fictional account of a family in therapy, Napier shows how each member of the family is involved when even one member is troubled, and how the trouble often stems from the relationship between father and mother.

Narramore, Bruce. *Why Children Misbehave.* Grand Rapids: Zondervan, 1980.

Nicholi, Armand M. "The Nontherapeutic Use of Psychoactive Drugs: A Modern Epidemic." *New England Journal of Medicine* 308 (April 1973): 925–933.

Norman, Jane and Myron Harris. *The Private Life of the American Teenager.* New York: Rawson, Wade Publishers, 1981.

Oates, Wayne E. *Pastoral Counseling in Grief and Separation.* Philadelphia: Fortress Press, 1976.

Offer, Daniel, Eric Ostrov, and I. Kenneth Howard. *The Adolescent: A Psychological Self-Portrait.* New York: Basic Books, 1981.

Olson, David H., and Hamilton I. McCubbin. *Families: What Makes Them Work.* Beverly Hills: Sage Publications, 1983.

Otto, Luther B. *How to Help Your Child Choose A Career.* New York: M. Evans and Company, 1984.

Otto, Mary L. "Child Abuse: Group Treatment for Parents." *Personnel and Guidance Journal* 62 (February 1984): 336–338.

Pasley, Kay, and Viktor Gecas. "Stresses and Satisfactions of the Parental Role." *Personnel and Guidance Journal* 62 (March 1984): 400–404.

Pogrebin, Letty Cottin. *Family Politics.* New York: McGraw-Hill, 1983.

Ray, Lynda Y. and Norbert Johnson. "Adolescent Suicide." *Personnel and Guidance Journal* 62 (November 1983): 132–133.

Reineke, Robert. Report to the National Board of American Lutheran Church Women on a Study of Attitudes of Women. Minneapolis: Search Institute, 1981.

Religion in America. Princeton: Princeton Religion Research Center, and Gallup Organization, 1981.

Religious Community and Chemical Health. Minneapolis: Minnesota Prevention Resource Center, 1983 Report.

Report on 1983 Minnesota Survey on Drug Use and Drug-Related Attitudes. Minneapolis: Search Institute, 1983.

Reuss, Carl F. *Profiles of Lutherans: An Interpretive Summary of an Inter-Lutheran Research Project.* Minneapolis: Augsburg Publishing, 1983.

Rice, Wayne. *Junior High Ministry.* Grand Rapids, MI: Zondervan, 1978. An honest and compassionate presentation of the difficulties of working with youth between the ages of twelve and fifteen, this book is as valuable for the parent as for the church youth worker.

Richards, Lawrence. "The Teacher as Interpreter of the Bible." *Religious Education* (September 1982): 515–516.

Ridenour, Fritz. *What Teenagers Wish Their Parents Knew About Kids.* Waco: Word Books, 1982. Informally, humorously written, this book helps parents to bridge the gap between their own thinking and that of their teenager. This author has used illustrations freely from his own family, not hesitating to show both the ups and downs of family life. Discussion questions follow each chapter.

Rosenthal, David. "The Year in the Movies." *Rolling Stone Yearbook* 25 (1983).

Rubenstein, Eli. "Television and Behavior: Research Conclusions of the 1982 NIMH Report and Their Policy Implications." *American Psychologist* (July 1983): 820–825.

Search Institute. *Young Adolescents and Their Parents Project Report.* Minneapolis: Search Institute, 1984.

Schuller, David S., Merton P. Strommen, et al. *Ministry in America.* San Francisco: Harper & Row, 1980.

Schuller, Robert H. *Self-Esteem: The New Reformation.* Waco: Word Books, 1982.

Shapiro, Philip. "A Treatment and Management Model." *Coping Magazine* (July 1983): 27–30.

Shedd, Charlie. *Promises to Peter.* Waco: Word Books, 1970.

Sheehy, Gail. "The Crisis Couples Face at 40." *McCall's* 103 (May 1976): 107.

Smith, Barbara. "Adolescent and Parent: Interaction Between Developmental Stages." *Quarterly Focus,* Center for Youth Development and Research (1976).

Straus, Murray. Family Patterns and Child Abuse in Nationally Representative American Sample. U.S. Government Publication Report reprinted in *Child Abuse and Neglect* 3, 1979.

Stromberg, Lee J. "Meet Hamilton McCubbin." *Correspondent* no. 520 (Winter 1983): 8, 9.

Strommen, Merton P. *A Call to Ministry.* Summary of 1981 Study Involving American Lutheran Church Women. Minneapolis: American Lutheran Church Women 1981.

Strommen, Merton P. *Five Cries of Youth.* New York: Harper & Row, 1974. This book makes use of research into high school age adolescents, revealing the cries of self-hatred, being a psychological orphan, social protests, prejudice, and joyous faith. The book, useful for personal reading or group discussion, has been effective in training youth leaders.

Strommen, Merton P., Milo L. Brekke, et al. *A Study of Generations.* Minneapolis: Augsburg Publishing, 1972.

Study of Work-Family Family Issues in Minnesota: An Educational Resource for the Business Community. Minnesota Department of Education, 1983.

Swanson, Steve. "Teen Suicide." *Lutheran Standard* 24 (February 3, 1984): 10–12.

Teenage Birth Rate Fact Sheet. Facts on Women Workers. U.S. Department of Labor, Office of the Secretary, Women's Bureau, 1982.

Tournier, Paul. *To Understand Each Other.* Richmond, Virginia: John Knox Press, 1962.

Varenhorst, Barbara B. *Real Friends: Becoming the Friend You'd Like to Have.* San Francisco: Harper & Row, 1983. Written by a nationally recognized authority on peer counseling, this heartwarming book shows how to become a friend. Parents will learn much about understanding and developing relationships with their own children through reading it, as well as learn a great deal about themselves. Adolescents will welcome it, since "how to make and keep friends" is a major concern of adolescence. It is written for young people in language they understand, and makes effective use of illustrations.

Walters, Richard P. *How to Be a Friend.* Ventura: Regal Books, 1981.

Watts, Judy Humphrey and Susan Lapinsky. "When Divorce Divides a Family." *Redbook* (April 1983): 67–69.

Weinstein, Grace W. "Should Teenagers Work?" *McCall's* (June 1983): 54–55.

Welter, Paul. *How to Help a Friend.* Wheaton, Illinois: Tyndale Press House Press, 1978.

Wenz, F. "Self-injury, Behavior, Economic Status and the Family Anomie Syndrome Among Adolescents." *Adolescence* 14, 387–397.

Wetzel, Laura and Mary Anne Ross. "Psychological and Social Ramifications of Battery: Observations Leading to a Counseling Methodology for Victims of Domestic Abuse." *Personnel and Guidance Journal* (March 1983), 423–427.

Wilt, Joy. *Raising Your Children Toward Emotional and Spiritual Maturity.* Waco: Word Books, 1977.

Wrenn, C. Gilbert. *The World of the Contemporary Counselor.* Boston: Houghton-Mifflin Company, 1973.

Wynne, Edward A. "Long-Term Trends Among Young Americans in Self- and Other Destructive Conduct." Paper presented at 1983 annual meeting of American Education Association, College of Education, Chicago.

"Youth and the Family." Center for Youth Development and Research, University of Minnesota Seminar Series #7 (September 1976).

Index